A Place of
Light and Love

~ WITNESSING HEAVEN ~

True Stories of Transformation from
Near-Death Experiences

A Place of
Light and Love

EDITORS OF GUIDEPOSTS

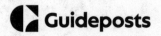

A Place of Light and Love

Published by Guideposts Books & Inspirational Media
100 Reserve Road, Suite E200
Danbury, CT 06810
Guideposts.org

Acknowledgments

Every attempt has been made to credit the sources of copyrighted material used in this book. If any such acknowledgment has been inadvertently omitted or miscredited, receipt of such information would be appreciated.

Scripture quotations marked (NIV) are taken from *The Holy Bible, New International Version*. Copyright © 1973, 1978, 1984, 2011 by Biblica, Inc. Used by permission of Zondervan. All rights reserved worldwide. zondervan.com

Scripture quotations marked (NKJV) are taken from *The Holy Bible, New King James Version*. Copyright © 1982 by Thomas Nelson.

Cover design by Pamela Walker, W Design Studio
Interior design by Pamela Walker, W Design Studio
Cover photo by Dreamstime
Typeset by Aptara, Inc.

ISBN 978-1-961125-79-7 (hardcover)
ISBN 978-1-961125-80-3 (epub)

Printed and bound in the United States of America

10 9 8 7 6 5 4 3 2 1

CONTENTS

INTRODUCTION

When we finally pass on from this world to the next, what awaits us? Departed family members? A choir of angels? A pastoral scene of lush fields, colorful flowers, and joyous people? As long as people have strived for heaven, they've wondered what it will be like. Can we even imagine something so wonderful? Over the years, writers, theologians, and philosophers have tried. Yet we can be assured of the glory of heaven from the testimonies of people who have experienced it firsthand.

Those who have had near-death experiences say that heaven is unequivocally real—and it is full of unimaginable wonder. In this book, four people share their account of heaven and shed light on the incredible peace, glory, and love that we can look forward to in the afterlife.

In each story in *A Place of Light and Love,* you'll read how a near-death experience dramatically changed the lives of those who witnessed the afterlife and returned to carry out the message they received while in heaven, to make God's plan the center of their lives.

We hope these stories of amazing heavenly encounters will give you comfort and peace in knowing that the eternal life promised to us in the Bible is real.

Dreams of Jesus—whom my mom had not yet started following—persisted for the remainder of her pregnancy. In one such dream, Mom saw herself bounding skyward in a big, white plane while standing beside Jesus. Luminous golden light poured through the windows, overcoming Mom with an all-consuming love. Even the love she had for me and my siblings, she says, could not compare to the extraordinary love that enveloped her in that fateful dream.

Seven months after her first dream of Jesus—and five days after Easter 2004—Mom delivered a perfectly healthy baby girl. There were no complications during the delivery. Doctors were understandably astonished; more shocking, my mom's health also began to inexplicably improve.

The light and love that my mom experienced in 2003 undoubtedly saved her life—and my little sister's life. Many who have had a near-death experience (NDE) say it is the light and love of Jesus that saved them as well.

Seeing "the Light"

Being enveloped by "the light" is one of the most well-documented aspects of an NDE. Men and women who have died and been resuscitated often recall being detached from their body, seeing their body from the outside, and entering a dazzling, bright light, sometimes through a dark tunnel. This blinding bright light, so beautiful and over-powering, is often described as being accompanied by an indescribable feeling of love.

In their case study, "Shedding Light on the Tunnel and Light in Near-Death Experiences," Janice Miner Holden and Saharnaz Loseu suggest that seeing "the light" during NDEs is not merely a biological phenomenon.[1] Although some researchers attribute this common NDE feature to hypoxia—that is, the reduced oxygen to the brain—or anoxia—the complete absence of oxygen in the brain—Holden and Loseu argue that something more is at play. Howard Smith, the NDE-er at the center of their case study, described himself as having been in a black void and witnessing a tunnel comprised of light. He characterized this light tunnel as a very bright white light that became focused—in the sense that everything else was black and he had no peripheral vision. He

> *The quality of the tunnel of light was nonthreatening, warm, and welcoming.*

further reported: "I simply looked down the tunnel at the light, and when I came to, I still had the memory of this light." He noted that although he did not recall the duration of time he spent in the tunnel, the memory of the tunnel was vivid for him after twenty years. Smith described the quality of the tunnel of light as nonthreatening, warm, and welcoming.

After ruling out all rational and scientific explanations for Howard's experience with "the light," Holden and Loseu learned that Howard came back with a "reassurance that consciousness continues after death, an increased sense of spirituality…and an openness to experiences that are not rationally justified."[2]

Accordingly, Leonard "Jay" Martin and Mike Olsen, whose powerful stories are detailed in this book, similarly came back with an increased sense of spirituality, describing having felt overcome by light and love during their astonishing near-death experiences. Jay says, "After my heavenly excursion, I was shot through with this fresh light and vision, bathed in love. It was universal, this great love! As soon as I got outside,

I was wowed. It was like it was a whole new world to me and nothing looked familiar."

Similarly, Mike recounts finding himself in a place of extraordinarily brilliant light. He writes, "I rocketed upward into a place of blinding white light—only it didn't blind me—it just transported me upward. The light seemed to go on forever. I felt the purest sense of peace I'd ever experienced as I approached what I knew was heaven." He concludes, "Now I can relax in God's love."

Now I can relax in God's love. What a comforting takeaway.

Love, Light, and NDEs

The Near-Death Experience Research Foundation (NDERF) was founded by Dr. Jeffrey Long, a practicing radiation oncologist, with the intention to document, research, and analyze the claims of NDE-ers across the world. With over four thousand stories on file, scientists at NDERF have found that people everywhere describe their experiences with remarkable similarity. In fact, while speaking to *Mysterious Ways* magazine,[3] Dr. Long asserted that NDE-ers often refer to being encompassed by a blinding, bright light and being overcome by a powerful feeling of love.

> For nearly everyone, they are overwhelmingly positive experiences. Many report seeing a bright light they might identify as a divine presence, as well as being surrounded by an all-encompassing feeling of love, beyond anything they've experienced on earth. Upward of 75 percent want to stay in the afterlife because of the love and joy they feel. As a result, nearly

100 percent no longer fear death. That's one of the most signifi-cant outcomes, an assurance that there is life after death.

In his bestselling book, *God and the Afterlife*, Dr. Long offers compel-ling testimonies from NDE-ers who felt enveloped by light and love while in heaven. Here are some of them.[4]

- I felt as if I had found the eternal fountain of love and I was splash-ing around in it. The overwhelming "vibe" from the beings of light was love. It almost felt like love was the glue holding everything together including myself.
- The feelings that radiated out from the light were full of unimag-inable love. I often close my eyes and try to remember all that happened so that I can once again experience that feeling.
- It was mind-blowing that this light was love…it was complete and unearthly. Such a strong feeling.
- I felt love flooding out of the bright light, encompassing everything. Beautiful!
- No human can ever love with the love I felt in that light. It is all-consuming and all-forgiving. Nothing matches it. It is like the day you looked into the eyes of your child for the first time, magnified a million times. Indescribable.
- There were no buildings, no structures, just light and love.
- I felt God's love as I was staring deep into the light.
- There was a magnificent Being of Light. He emanated not just light but love as well: an amazing amount of love.
- The love I felt in the light had no attendant worries, just love, joy, and light. When I held my sons, I burst into delighted laughter

A Luminous Love

By Sadashaya Maitlall

Every moment is made glorious by the light of love.

Rumi, thirteenth-century Persian poet

This was not quite a near-death experience, but it sure comes close.

The year was 2003, and my mom was sick. *Very* sick. Her kidneys were failing, her heart was enlarged, and her blood pressure was dangerously high. To make matters more complicated, doctors could not find the root cause of Mom's ailments and therefore could not provide her with a certain prognosis.

Despite the situation, Mom soldiered on—thanks to her dedication to me and my sisters, who were all under the age of ten. She was still able to function in her everyday life—and continued to be a devoted wife and mother—though it was not without some real struggle.

Then, in the summer of that same year, Mom received some shocking news.

She was *pregnant*.

My mom could not believe it. She had not been trying for a child— she and Dad already had four—and, up until then, had believed her age (she was in her late thirties) and poor health had lowered her chances of conceiving again.

Taking my mom's poor health into account, as well as the troublesome fact that she had already had four cesarean sections because of her petite stature, doctors were convinced that she and the baby would not survive the delivery. They encouraged her to not move forward with the pregnancy.

Devastated, my mom questioned her faith. Where was God when she needed Him? A few weeks later she would have a dream—and a chance to meet Him, face-to-face.

> *Jesus shone a radiant white light from His eyes over Mom's body.*

In the dream Mom was awakened in the middle of the night by a knock at our front door. When she padded on bare feet down the stairs and cautiously peeked through a window—fearing who it could be at such a late hour—she was shocked to see Jesus standing on our stoop, gesturing for her to invite Him inside.

Though my mom stubbornly refused to let Him in, upset at God for her current situation, Jesus was invited inside by my dad, who'd just come home from work in the dream. My mom was stunned—and then the unthinkable happened.

While standing in our living room, Jesus shone a radiant white light from His eyes over Mom's body and over that of a baby sitting at her feet.

Mom awoke the next morning to discover that her blood pressure was deathly high. Doctors said she could have died that night and were shocked that she had somehow managed to pull through.

The city does not need the sun or the moon to shine on it, for the glory of God gives it light, and the Lamb is its lamp.

Revelation 21:23 (NIV)

with each of them. That joy was so similar to what I felt in the light.

Dr. Long ultimately concludes that "Love is clearly an important part of near-death experiences. This experience of deep love often carries within it an affirmation of unity or oneness between all people or even all things." He adds that his findings lend commentary not only on death but also on life itself. He explains, "These transformative experiences of a unique love—a love that is total, unconditional, and enormous—speak not just to what happens after we die, but to what matters *while we live*. These people described their encounters with death, but the message, instead, is one about the meaning of life."[5]

Love is an important part of near-death experiences.

Therefore, the main takeaway of near-death experiences—at least for Dr. Long—is that as long as we are alive, we are meant to love. And, as so many near-death experiencers have pointed out in their testimonies, God made us with a unique purpose: to give and receive His love.

Is the Light a Person?

Interestingly, for many NDE-ers, the all-loving light they encounter in heaven is not merely something they feel. It's some*one*.

In his study titled "The Significance of Light in the Near-Death Experience," physician Thomas Lee Baumann, the author of *God at the Speed of Light: The Melding of Science and Spirituality*, argues that the blinding light that near-death experiencers claim to have seen in the afterlife may be God Himself.[6] Dr. Baumann explains:

> Light has long been recognized as a principal characteristic of the near-death experience (NDE). However, its significance has been widely debated. [My study] details the significance of light in the NDE, and it further suggests that science supports the contention that the light of the NDE represents the presence of a loving and concerned Creator. I cite well-established and celebrated physics experiments to support the argument that light exhibits supernatural—even conscious—qualities. The relationship of light to the NDE, quantum physics, and descriptions of God throughout the world's literature serves to illuminate the argument that God and the light may well be one and the same.

The light that near-death experiencers see and feel in heaven is a manifestation of God's love.

Dr. Baumann goes on to explain in depth how light, like God, is omnipresent, omniscient, omnipotent, and even conscious. According to him, the light that near-death experiencers see and feel in heaven is, undoubtedly, a manifestation of God's love.

NDE-er Andrew "Andy" Petro, the author of *Alive in the Light: Remembering Eternity* and whose NDE has been documented by Dr. Long, describes at length his fascinating experience with a personified "Light" in the afterlife.[7] He writes:

> I looked directly into the source of the Light and it appeared to me in a human-like form. It looked like a massive human silhouette

that was radiating with the brightness of a thousand suns. Although I couldn't remember seeing its form before, somehow I recognized it. The Light spoke to me: "Andy, do not be afraid. Andy, I love you. Andy, we love you."…

Then after what seemed like hours in the sphere, I was instantly back in the tunnel again, drawn toward the Light. I could actually feel its brightness, warmth, and love. As I got closer to the Light, I was absorbed by its brilliance and perfect love.

I was in the Light! Oh my God, I was actually in the Light. I was the Light!

For Andy, the Light was a person—a person who loves him profoundly. "The Light also knew everything that I have ever done or will do," he explains, "and the Light loved me without conditions. The Light loved me because of who I am—Andy, a piece of the Light. There was no fear. No judgment. No punishment. No blame. No shame. No ledger of good and bad deeds. I was one with the unconditionally loving Light. I was home. I was home forever."[8]

Similarly, Leonard "Jay" Martin, who also shared his amazing near-death experience with NDERF, encountered a light that had human-like features and filled him with an intense feeling of love.[9] This "light being," according to him, is all-knowing and all-loving. He tells NDERF:

At some point, I felt sucked away into a long dark tunnel at an incredible speed! At the tunnel end there was a glowing pinpoint…. The more I went forward, the more the light grew. I arrived into this light. The light was wonderful and very bright. But what hit me the most is that in this light I felt at peace, joy, but most of all I felt an incredible love! This light loved me! This light talked to me! I asked it if it was God and it answered me, "Yes I am the light!" This light being (whom I did not see) knew EVERYTHING about me.

In Jay's experience, God and the light are one and the same. It is through the light that God conveys His warm and powerful personality and communicates His deep and profound love.

Light and Love in Scripture

In the Bible, God is repeatedly identified as both light and love. In the Gospel of John, for instance, Jesus famously says, "I am the light of the world. Whoever follows me will never walk in darkness, but will have the light of life" (John 8:12, NIV). In 1 John 4:8, John the Apostle pointedly states that "God is love." He explains:

> *In the Bible, God is repeatedly identified as both light and love.*

This is how God showed his love among us: He sent his one and only Son into the world that we might live through him. This is love: not that we loved God, but that he loved us and sent his Son as an atoning sacrifice for our sins. Dear friends, since God so loved us, we also ought to love one another. No one has ever seen God; but if we love one another, God lives in us and his love is made complete in us. (1 John 4:9–11, NIV)

Though we cannot conclude definitively if the light NDE-ers like Andy, Jay, Chantal, and David encountered is truly God, it makes sense why heaven would be a place of love and light. After all, if heaven is God's abode, and "God is love" and Jesus "is the light," then heaven would surely be encompassed with all things light and love.

Julie Papievis and Sharlene Spires, who share their astonishing near-death accounts in this book, describe their incredible experience of seeing "the light" and recognizing it as God's love.

"As this penetrating light surrounded me," writes Julie, "I was shocked by its physical warmth. I felt as if it was gathering me in its arms to comfort me and to reassure me that everything would be okay. I also sensed that if I walked into this blue light, it would lead to eternity. I couldn't stop staring into this light. Somehow I knew it was the presence of the Lord's holiness. It was…pure love…"

Similarly, Sharlene explains that a dazzling, bright light—and a powerful feeling of love—permeated heaven. She recalls:

> [The Light] contained…an abundance of love. There was more love than I had ever experienced or ever knew existed. I was filled up to the brim, overflowing. This love reached everywhere inside of my being, my spiritual being…This love was the greatest emotion I had ever felt. It reached hidden places that I didn't even know about. Places deep inside of my soul—empty places that I had been longing to be filled my entire life. …
>
> I do not know how long I was in that Light—it seemed like such a long time, even though time was not measured in that realm. I only know it felt like forever, and I wanted it to be forever.
>
> I started to think about Jesus. As I did, I was drawn further into the Light. …

I stood in front of this magnificent, ancient tree and watched the Light swirl around. I let it wash over me. I felt the love of Heavenly Father still with me. Moments passed as I basked in the Light and love."

Receiving God's Light and Love

Julie and Sharlene's near-death accounts bear striking similarity to John the Evangelist's description of heaven, where light is eternal and all-encompassing. According to the book of Revelation, Jesus is heaven's greatest source of light. While envisioning the heavenly hereafter, in fact, John the Evangelist offers a glorious image of a world that is lit by God. He poignantly writes, "There will be no more night. They will not need the light of a lamp or the light of the sun, for the Lord God will give them light. And they will reign for ever and ever" (Revelation 22:5, NIV).

> *According to the book of Revelation, Jesus is heaven's greatest source of light.*

End Notes

1. Janice Holden Miner, Janice and Saharnaz Loseu, "Shedding Light on the Tunnel and Light in Near-Death Experiences: A Case Study," https://digital.library.unt.edu/ark:/67531/metadc948094/m2/1/high_res_d/34-1%205.%20Holden%20cx%202018.pdf.

2. Ibid.

3. The Editors of Guideposts, "A Conversation with a Near-Death Experience Expert," https://guideposts.org/angels-and-miracles/a-conversation-with-a-near-death-experience-expert-2/.

4. NDERF, "Love Encountered in Near-Death Experiences," https://www.nderf.org/Hub/love.htm.

5. Jeffrey Long, "Stories of God's love common among those who almost die, says doctor who studies them," https://www.washingtonpost.com/news/acts-of-faith/wp/2016/06/29/people-who-had-near-death-experiences-consistently-report-one-thing-gods-love/.

6. T. Lee Baumann, "The Significance of Light in the Near-Death Experience," https://digital.library.unt.edu/ark:/67531/metadc799019/m2/1/high_res_d/vol23-no4-197.pdf.

7. NDERF, "Andrew P NDE" https://www.nderf.org/Experiences/1andrew_p_nde.html.

8. Ibid.

9. NDERF, "Leonard NDE" https://www.nderf.org/Experiences/1leonard_nde.html.

Making Every Breath Count

By Mike Olsen

*The Spirit of God has made me; the breath
of the Almighty gives me life.*

Job 33:4 (NIV)

"Mike, we found a match," my doctor said over the phone. "You're getting a new set of lungs. I'll see you in surgery early tomorrow morning."

I stared at my wife, Patti, in shock. I could hardly believe what I was hearing. This was the call we'd been praying for. I hung up the phone, and Patti swept me into a hug.

Five years before, I'd been diagnosed with idiopathic pulmonary fibrosis (IPF), a disease that causes scar tissue to form in the lungs, making it hard to breathe. There is no cure and, in some cases, like mine, no known cause. I'd been on the transplant list for four years, each night wondering if I would wake up the next morning.

This was the news we'd been waiting for—a message of hope and a future. Little did I know how much this call would change my life.

Finding God

I grew up in an abusive household and went to Catholic school as a kid. Most days were rough between the abuse at home and the nuns at school. I did, however, first learn of God at school and developed a relationship with Him, though that relationship was more in my head than in my heart.

During those years I developed a love of singing and acting and ended up at The New School in New York City for college. I was actually pretty good and even signed with an agent to help me break into the acting scene in New York City. One day a friend from Parsons School of Design was stabbed in front of a bar. I was shaken. As I said, I knew of God but I wasn't living as a Christian. Things changed that day. I found a church with people who welcomed me and accepted me without judgment. I learned about the love of Jesus, and eventually I gave my life to Him.

I was nineteen and pursuing my acting career when God asked me to give up acting.

I was nineteen and pursuing my acting career when God asked me to give up acting. Did I hear right? Didn't He know this was my passion? What would I do for a living? I wasn't sure but I followed His request. I quit acting and started working in Soho for a stationery company. After that I found other work to pay the bills, but nothing I was trained for or really interested in. Eventually God called me to ministry and I ended up enrolling in Bible college.

After college I was working and attending church in New Jersey, still wondering what God wanted me to do with my life. It's there I met

Patti. She had been living in Guatemala with her family, ministering to people in need, unsure what she would do with her life. The pastor at this New Jersey church asked her to come help out. She knew the pastor's son from the mission field, so she agreed to come up.

"That girl is cute," I told my friend after I met Patti. I even jokingly said, "I'm gonna marry her one day." I'm not sure Patti was all that interested in me, though. She said she was sick of guys and didn't want to date. I didn't let that stop me. One day I said, "Hey, Patti. You're new here. I want to take you to this concert in Manhattan. We're all going as a group." A bunch of us from church were thinking about going to hear John Michael Talbot, a Catholic monk who plays classical guitar. She reluctantly agreed, and then I called up my buddies and said, "Hey, you wouldn't like it. Just a boring old monk." I whittled down the group one by one until it was just me and Patti.

So I went to pick her up, red rose in hand. She took one look at just me and said, "Where is everybody?"

"Oh, they couldn't come so it's just us," I told her.

She was not happy! After spending a quiet evening together she was adamant we would be just friends. Shortly after, I started attending Bible college in Rhode Island and she eventually moved to Staten Island. We began dating after three years of being friends, were engaged not too long after, and got married just three months later.

We were living in Bloomington, Indiana, when I felt God's nudge to start my pastoring career by being a youth minister. I was blessed with three opportunities—one in Louisville, Kentucky, another in St. Louis, Missouri, and a third in Florida. These were all new areas to us, and none was near family. Patti and I prayed and decided to take the position in Louisville, which also came with housing. So Patti and I packed our belongings in a small U-Haul and drove to Louisville. We arrived to find out the church had changed their minds! So there we were in a new city with no jobs and no place to live.

Any other person might have said, "What the heck?" But Patti and I turned to God. "Okay, Lord. What are we gonna do?" We ended up living in a deacon's basement. Patti took a job as a nanny while I started working at a drapery company. We eventually had enough money to get an apartment.

You'd think we would have had nothing to do with that church after turning us away with no notice. But we were part of that congregation for two years, until I was ordained as an Anglican priest and started preaching at a small parish. The congregation of this new church was mostly older folks. The church wasn't growing, especially since I was burying a number of parishioners, but I was enjoying pastoring here and Patti and I liked being involved in our lively worship services: Patti played the piano and I sang.

I thought we should move closer to family, but I heard the Lord say to stay where we were.

One day I thought we should move closer to family, but I heard the Lord say to stay where we were. So we did—and just a few weeks later I was diagnosed with IPF. I'm positive it's no coincidence that the University of Louisville and Jewish Hospital Trager Transplant Center is only five minutes away. God knew what He was doing!

A Surprising Diagnosis

In 2012 I started having lung trouble after a terrible ice storm in Kentucky. Our power lines were down for two weeks. We couldn't even make it to our jobs during that time. My wife, our dogs, and I slept on a mattress in front of the woodstove in the living room. We huddled around it all day while linemen worked around the clock to get electricity back.

After the storm, a persistent hacking cough convinced me I needed to see a doctor. I knew this was more than a simple cold. One morning after my coughing had kept me and Patti awake all night, Patti drove me to the emergency room. Turns out, I'd developed pneumonia. The doctor gave me antibiotics and I didn't give it much thought. I figured the meds would do their job and fix my lungs.

I knew this was more than a simple cold. Turns out, I'd developed pneumonia.

When they sent me home with the doctor's report, I stuck it in my jacket pocket, not bothering to read that the doctor had written, "Looks like pulmonary fibrosis." By the time I came across those papers two years later, it was too late—the damage had been done.

Up until this time I was a healthy fifty-four-year-old. I'd never smoked a day in my life. I'd been singing since I was a child and had even performed at the Emerson Little Theater in New Jersey. Patti and I ate a very healthy diet. But over the next two years following that trip to the ER, my breathing became more and more labored. I thought I'd developed allergies.

In 2013 my allergist said, "Mike, you're suffering from more than allergies to grass or pollen. You're here in my office a couple times a year with bronchitis or another lung issue. We can't keep prescribing more and more rounds of antibiotics for you." He told me he was sending me to a pulmonologist.

The pulmonologist took X-rays and scans, then told me it looked like I had IPF. But they needed to verify that diagnosis with an open lung biopsy, where they remove and analyze a small piece of lung. After the biopsy the pulmonologist called me into his office and said, "Mike, this is very serious." Then he told me I had only about two years to live.

My condition deteriorated rapidly until I needed to be on oxygen 24/7. I started having to drag my oxygen tank up to the pulpit. Speaking became difficult and at times I could hardly stand. I had been preaching at this church for seventeen years but it became too much, so I closed the doors.

A Different Kind of Preaching

I was in shock when I was first diagnosed. I mean, I was healthy. I was young.

I went to the place I liked to go to talk to God—my backyard chapel. I'd converted it from a dance studio after my son, Chauncey, moved out a few years before, and it had become my place of solitude. As a pastor, I'd found I needed a place to pray, and this was a special place. I had set it up with the Catholic stations of the cross and other altarpieces I had. I've even held church services in this chapel followed by a back-yard picnic.

Today, it was time for a "come to Jesus meeting."

Two years left. I figured I had three options: wait for a miracle from God, get a transplant, or die. I knew God performed miracles, so that wasn't out of the question. After that conversation with the doctor, I was immediately added to the transplant list, so receiving a new set of lungs was a possibility. Dying? I would be okay with that, though I didn't want to leave my family.

I turned to God. I told Him I wasn't going to ask why me. I know things happen to people all the time. Life is hard. Sometimes we all have to deal with the unexpected. But I needed to know what He wanted me to do. That's when I heard Him say: "Trust Me." At that moment a supernatural peace came over me.

> *I needed to know what He wanted me to do. That's when I heard Him say: "Trust Me."*

I missed pastoring, engaging with people. And that's when I decided to start the Mike Olsen Project, a grassroots organization to raise awareness of IPF. I figured I'd come into this world crying, kicking, and screaming and I'd leave the same way. I was determined that people know about IPF and the need for a cure. I started making noise.

I was shocked to discover that the American Lung Association (ALA) had no information on its website about this deadly disease that kills almost as many people as breast cancer. I found the phone number for the head of the ALA and called him. Surprisingly, he answered. We talked, and I told him about my struggles with IPF and how people needed information and we needed to find a cure. He told me he would bring this up at a meeting. I'm pretty sure he listened because soon after that meeting, I discovered a section of information about IPF posted on the lung association's website.

I knocked on more doors. I reached out to my local and state politicians. They're supposed to be representing me, right? I even sent a message to our President and told him something needed to be done for Americans dying from this disease. Three days after we talked, he signed the Right to Try Act, a way for terminally ill patients who have tried all approved treatment options to access investigational treatment options. I'm not sure if my big mouth made a difference, but I felt like I was starting to gain traction in my campaign.

I met with celebrities. I started writing magazine articles, appearing on TV shows, and taking part in podcasts. I talked to doctors and hospitals about doing more for IPF patients and treatments. I also did a lot of public speaking to students and faculty at medical universities.

During this same time, I got a call from Gilbert Corsey, a reporter with WDRB Louisville, about my story. In December 2016 and for a full year after, he followed me, recording my journey of living with IPF. The documentary was called "I'm Dying, Will You Help?"

Gilbert called with the exciting news that we were nominated for an Emmy Award. He invited me and Patti to the awards show, so we got all dressed up and walked the red carpet. What a night. I was doing something I'd been dreaming about for years, though my dream had included being nominated for my acting.

When "I'm Dying, Will You Help?" won, Gilbert went up on stage to accept the award. He called out to me to come up on stage with him. As he handed me the award, he said, "Mike, this is your award. It's your story. Your name is engraved here. It belongs to you." He even asked me, right there on stage, to address the Emmy crowd. I looked up to heaven and said, "God, You really have a sense of humor." Many years before, God had asked me to give up a stage career to pursue ministry. And now He was awarding me an Emmy not for acting but for dying. It was a full-circle moment for me.

As part of the Mike Olsen Project I also started a Facebook page to connect with fellow IPF sufferers. I posted a message that I was available to talk with anyone who needed a listening ear, even though I, too, was suffering. This outreach helped fill my days with significance and, hopefully, will make a positive difference for people suffering from the disease who have no hope or spirituality.

I hate that I had to give up the pulpit, but I was still able to preach—just to a bigger and different audience as I brought awareness to IPF.

The Call That Changed My Life

I'm getting a lung transplant," I said aloud, still in disbelief.

We packed a bag and hurried to the car, my oxygen tank in tow. During the drive to the hospital, I was lost in thought. Receiving a new pair of lungs was a huge blessing, but it was a lot for me to take in. Even though my lungs were no longer healthy, it was hard to reconcile losing the organs I'd used to take my first breath, sing my first song. They were about to be replaced by the lungs of a total stranger, an anonymous donor, someone whose death meant that my life would be saved. I felt guilty that I got to keep on living and deeply disconnected from the stranger's lungs that would allow me to do so. It felt as if I were taking something that didn't belong to me.

I knew one potential risk of surgery was that my body could reject the new lungs. I couldn't help but wonder—if my mind couldn't come to terms with the transplant what chance did my body have? Though I tried to push the question from my mind, it needled me like a thorn.

At the hospital Patti and I settled in and waited for the operation, which was scheduled for 6 a.m. In the morning, the nurses prepped me for surgery. I kissed Patti and held her close. "Everything is going to be okay," she said. Still, as the nurses got me ready, I remained uneasy. When they wheeled me into the operating room and put the anesthesia mask over my face, I sank into darkness.

Suddenly, I was conscious. I couldn't feel anything, but I could see. *What's going on?* I thought. I was in the operating room, but I wasn't on the operating table—I was floating above it. From my vantage point overhead I saw my body on the table. The surgeons were hunched over my body, conferring with one another. I thought something must have gone very wrong.

I kept rising upward until the scene below me disappeared and I came to a space of swirling rainbow-colored lights. *That must be some strong anesthesia*, I thought. I'd never done hard drugs but figured this was what that must be like. It was pretty wild. Somehow I knew I was in heaven.

I was in the operating room, but I wasn't on the operating table—I was floating above it.

Reds, blues, green, yellows, all spun together in a mesmerizing display. The lights were comforting, as if beckoning me to follow. As I moved along, I heard a droning noise, sort of like the sound you hear when bagpipes are playing. A dull consistent noise. But this noise wasn't annoying—it was beautiful. Then that droning turned into melodic singing. Singing voices. The melody was enchanting, but I couldn't make out the words. That is, until a chorus of voices announced over the singing: "Mike's coming home!" The angels knew my name! God knew my name!

My upbringing had taught me that God was "up there" with a hammer, that He didn't like you. For much of my life I'd heard I wasn't good enough. But here, bathed in this incredible technicolor light, I felt total freedom. No fear, no guilt. Here, there were no mistakes, no shortcomings, no bad things. I felt complete, in sync with this light, with God.

> *I felt pure peace and joy. I'd never experienced such bliss before.*

Then I heard a commanding voice say, "No. He's just here for a visit."

In a sudden burst of energy I was transported to a place of blinding white light. It surrounded me and stretched on endlessly. I felt only pure peace and joy. I'd never experienced such bliss before. I was in heaven but as that divine voice had said, I was only there for a visit.

Part of my finite mind remembered where I'd been—in the OR, getting a double lung transplant. And in my mind I thought about my donor. I realized someone had sacrificed for me. I knew what I needed to do. I called out into the light—not with my voice but with my soul: "I want to thank my organ donor."

A presence materialized behind my left shoulder. I turned and saw two figures approaching. I could see only the outline of their forms, shimmering and iridescent. I recognized one as Jesus and the other alongside him as my anonymous donor.

"Thank you," I communicated. With every bit of my essence, I exuded pure gratitude. "Thank you."

I sensed that the donor accepted my gratitude with humility. Jesus then put His hand on my shoulder.

"There are your lungs now," He said.

"Yes," I replied.

With that, I fell backward, the space of light turning into a speck before disappearing entirely. For a moment I was back in my body on the operating table at the hospital, until everything went black.

My New Reality

I later learned that I'd been in a coma for ten days. During the transplant, the first lung went in fine. After the second lung was put in, the surgeon released a clamp too early. I'd bled out and needed to be resuscitated. Only through the staff's best efforts had I been brought back. I was hooked up to a machine that breathed for me until I regained consciousness. Despite everything that had happened, the transplant was successful. I had my new lungs.

The road to recovery has been long and hard. When you sign up for a transplant, you're essentially trading one disease for another. I needed weekly surgeries to clean my lungs for the first few months. Then I started going in for monthly blood tests to make sure my body wasn't rejecting the organs. I've had seventy surgical procedures since my transplant, and I take twenty-seven pills every day to stay alive.

Patti has been a godsend. She grew up in a godly family, with a dad who was a doctor and a mom who was a nurse. She spent a lot of time with her family in Guatemala, ministering to the sick there and sometimes holding the hand of people her dad was operating on. She also worked in her dad's office, so she grew up hearing medical terms and seeing doctor-patient interactions. She was trained early on to accept whatever God puts in your path and has been my advocate and caregiver since my diagnosis.

I'm still disabled because of all the bronchial stenosis, a common complication after lung transplantation. I can't work and that's tough for me, but I've taken on the role of housekeeper and do what I can before Patti gets home from work.

Sharing My Story

People contact me all the time from all over the world; I've sort of become the poster boy for IPF. But I don't mind. I know this is part of God's plan for me.

One time, a guy named Mark saw my story and called me. He'd just gotten diagnosed with IPF as a result of having had COVID-19. We talked about how he was feeling, what he was doing. I could tell from talking to him that something wasn't quite right. I asked him how many liters of oxygen he was on. I told him I could tell just from listening to him that I thought he needed more. I encouraged him to go back to his pulmonologist. He was like, "Yeah, I will," but he didn't. I continued telling him to go after he continued telling me about the trouble he was having.

He lived near Tampa, and I knew Tampa General was a transplant facility. For whatever reason he didn't talk to his doctor or go to the hospital, until finally one day his oxygen saturation dropped into the fifties. A normal level is over 95 percent. He went to the emergency room and was so bad that he ended up being put on the transplant list. Just a few weeks later he received a double lung transplant. I was floored. What if I hadn't been there for him?

This was not the first time something like this has happened. I feel like I almost have a whole other line of business, an advocate on call. IPF sufferers are coming to me to help them understand what they should expect with the disease, but I'm also a breath of hope for people. While I share information about IPF, I also take every opportunity to share about my visit to heaven and putting our trust in God.

Another time I was traveling and started chatting to a woman at the hotel where I was staying. As she was checking me in we got to talking about IPF and my transplant. I also told her about my NDE, going to heaven, and talking to Jesus. By the end

> *I'm a breath of hope for people. I take every opportunity to share about my visit to heaven.*

of it she was weeping. I told her I was sorry I made her cry, but she was grateful. That day she had been questioning whether there was a heaven, and there I was, telling her heaven is real. I know that was no coincidence.

My entire life is an open book. I'm not ashamed of any of it, including the abuse I suffered. One time, when Patti and I were in Holland doing street ministry, I got an opportunity to share that part of my story. Patti received a divine message. She told me I needed to talk to a girl who was sitting across the street on the curb. "You need to tell her your story of abuse," she said. So I approached this girl and started talking to her. I told her I had been abused when I was a kid. She started crying. Her dad had been abusing her for years and she'd never told anyone. She said my opening up to her let her know it was okay to talk about it.

This girl who had been suffering in silence was addicted to heroin and felt hopeless and helpless. I have stayed in contact with both the local pastor there as well as this young woman. She's done a complete turnaround. She's no longer using drugs and she attends church. This is just one more example of how God is using me to share with others what I've gone through as a way to help and support them.

He is using Patti too. She's been working at her bank for over twenty years, so she knows a lot of the customers. People tell her their woes— she's sort of like a bartender in that way. But they also ask about me and how I'm doing. She uses these opportunities to tell them how I died on the table during my transplant, went to heaven, and came back.

Changed in More Ways Than One

Nothing on earth compares to being in heaven. Patti noticed the change in me; my sister did, too, and so have our friends.

> *I got a taste of heaven, and each time I share my story it's as if I'm there again.*

I used to like antiquing, going to flea markets and Goodwill, and using my creative side to make new things. Some of that desire is still there, but it doesn't mean the same to me now. In fact, very little means the same. I got a taste of heaven, the place I know is my destiny, and each time I share my story it's as if I'm there again.

I love my wife; we've been married for over thirty-five years. I love my son. I love taking care of my family. But it's hard being back, especially because I suffer every day.

During the years we've spent in Louisville we've developed a great circle of close friends—some we've known for more than twenty-five years. After my transplant, some of them walked away from our relationship. I don't blame them. I'm a lot to deal with. I have a bunch of food restrictions, so going to someone's house for dinner has its challenges. People are also concerned about germs, which I'm grateful for. Before COVID, they might have worried they could give me a cold or the flu; now, they worry they could pass along something that could kill me.

I'm not complaining, though. While some people don't know how to handle chronic illness and suffering, others look to me for inspiration. As I get older, I realize my time on earth gets shorter and shorter—especially for me. The transplant center gave me five years. At the time of this writing, I'm on year four. Some double lung transplant patients live longer, but those are typically younger people. I was fifty-seven when I received my transplant.

No matter how much time I have left before returning to my eternal home, I will continue to share my experiences. I feel like when Jesus touched me and told me the lungs were mine and to receive them, He wanted me to go back and share with others all the amazing things God does.

People have been changed, but I have too. Right now I just look for opportunities to be a light wherever I go—using the light that touched me in heaven to touch other people through me. I minister to people to help them prevail regardless of the odds. God continues to tell me to "trust Him," as He directs my life so I can make every breath count.

My Life since My Near-Death Experience

Mike Olsen

I've always been an optimist, even during my tough upbringing. I think even then I kind of knew God was with me, that He was training me to cling to Him. No matter what life has thrown at me, I've learned to make lemonade out of lemons—or in my case, to make every breath count.

Q *Do you ever think about what your life might have been like if you'd become an actor?*

A I do. It was hard giving up acting when I was nineteen. I really like it and was good at it. But I wonder if I'd gone down that road if I'd be the same person I am today.

Years ago, when I was a young guy, I went to a bar in Manhattan frequented by people from the theater district. A producer came up to me and told me if I slept around, I'd probably get the parts I wanted. That solidified it for me and I walked away.

I sometimes wonder if I would have made it. But I also wonder if I would be a Christian if I'd gone to Hollywood. Would I be compassionate? Would I be the person I am today? Would I have this disease? My life has been enriched by so many other things because of my Christian journey. God has taken me to many beautiful places, and I've been able to meet some incredible people along the way. I've been enriched by people from all over the world.

Q *What do you think God meant when He told you those lungs were yours now?*

A God gave me those lungs for a reason, so I focus on being healthy so I can live my new life to the fullest. I continue working in ministry while also advocating for funding studies about IPF. I can even sing again. Patti says I'm like the words in the Tim McGraw song, "Live Like You Were Dying." My sister called recently and told me it's like I've come alive. I figure no matter how much time I have on earth, I can help people along the way.

My intention when I started the Mike Olsen Project was to create a foundation that can assist patients and their families who are dealing with the disease. I want to not only raise awareness of IPF but also provide financial assistance to patients undergoing treatment, share research and medical opportunities, and offer emotional and spiritual support.

Q *Have you had any contact with the family of your lung donor?*

A I pray for my donor's family often, especially on my "lungaversary"—January 7. While I celebrate life because of my new lungs, I wonder what they are doing, how they are remembering their loved one. I wrote them, acknowledging the incredible gift of organ donation, but I haven't heard from them yet. I would love to tell them what I saw while I was in heaven, but I'm not sure I'll ever have that opportunity.

Q *What do you think when you look at your Emmy Award?*

A The Emmy Award sits on the piano in our living room. I also have a wall of remembrance in our bedroom. It includes pictures of me with politicians and celebrities; a framed certificate from when I was named a Kentucky Colonel, an honor awarded by the governor to civilians who have made outstanding contributions, service, or accomplishments to a community, the state, or the nation; the key to the city of Louisville, which was presented to me by the mayor; copies of magazine articles featuring my story; and more.

All this stuff, all these accolades, makes me chuckle. So many years ago I was hoping for accolades for my acting career. Instead, I've received awards and recognition because of my disease.

The Light of His Love

By Sharlene Spires, as told to Stephanie Thompson

The sun will no more be your light by day, nor will the brightness of the moon shine on you, for the Lord *will be your everlasting light, and your God will be your glory.*

Isaiah 60:19 (NIV)

Since I was a girl, I've searched for love. True love. Unconditional love. I often watched fairy tales like *Cinderella* and *Sleeping Beauty,* dreaming of the day my own handsome prince would swoop in, rescue me, and fill me up with the love I craved. In my naive, romantic heart I believed this prince would be the answer to my desperate yearning for love. Happily-ever-after seemed far away in the future, but as a child in the 1970s, it was my ultimate goal.

Growing up I always felt like an outsider looking in at other people living their lives. I never seemed to fit in anywhere. I believed something was flawed about me. I was desperate to be accepted and loved for just who I was.

Even after I married my husband, Mike, in 1991 and felt entirely loved by him, I still had an empty space, a niggling deep down in my soul that the love I possessed was not enough. I wanted and needed more. I felt incomplete—like working an entire puzzle only to find a piece missing once it was finished.

It wasn't until October 2020, during one of the most difficult seasons of my life, that I received the love I'd yearned for. This love finally filled the empty place inside my soul. Through an amazing encounter, that missing puzzle piece found me, and I met my one true Prince. My story has a happy ending, and now I am whole.

Mimi's Girl

I'm the eldest of four daughters. Mom was young, only seventeen, when I was born. My father was six years older than she was and worked as a residential frame carpenter in South Florida. A year and a half after I was born, my sister Cindy came along. Three years later, Shannon was born, and four years after that, Cathy.

Mother was the second to the youngest of six children. Since Mom started a family as a teen, she depended heavily on her mother, who was by then a widow. From the time I was a baby, I was often over at Mimi's. We lived right down the road, so every day after my dad would go to work, Mom would strap me in a stroller and walk me down to Mimi's house. We'd stay there until late afternoon. Sometimes I'd stay with Mimi while Mom went home to start supper, then my mother would pick me up later.

Mimi always greeted us at the door. Her beautiful blue Irish eyes lit up with joy as she pulled me close, hugged me tight, and kissed me on the forehead after I stepped inside. A physically demonstrative person, she often took hold of my hands when she talked to me. She had many loving, sweet, physical gestures. She often brushed the hair off my fore-head when I was in her presence.

Even though I was young, I remember the ways Mimi spoiled me. She gave me a pacifier dipped in sugar and hid away a bottle for me, even after I was weaned. She'd fill it with sugar water, and I'd suck on it all day until we heard my mom come in, then we'd run and hide it away. It was a little game we played, and I loved that we had a secret between just the two of us. Even though Mimi was sweet and loving to all of her fifteen grandchildren, she and I had a special bond. I wasn't her first grandchild, but I was the first one to live so physically close to her. Since I saw her nearly every day, we grew very close emotionally.

Even though Mimi was sweet and loving to all of her grandchildren, she and I had a special bond.

A petite and slender woman, Mimi stood a mere four foot ten inches tall. By the time I was in middle school I had grown taller than she was. She had the brightest eyes I ever did see. Her soft, curly brown hair was coiffed at the beauty salon each week, like most women of her generation. She wore dresses and heels, and a head scarf over her hair. She always had a pretty handbag in the crook of her arm if she was going somewhere. I wanted to be just like her, so as a preschooler I would only wear dresses. I wanted a scarf in my hair nearly every day, too, so I would be like Mimi.

By the time I started elementary school, my family had moved to Rolling Oaks, a prominent neighborhood on the edge of the Everglades in Fort Lauderdale—thirty minutes away from Mimi. But even with this distance Mom still visited her mother nearly every day. She signed me up for school using Mimi's address so I could attend near her neigh-borhood. Mom would make the drive every morning, drop me off at school, then spend the day at Mimi's with my sisters. She'd usually walk to pick me up and then we'd stay at Mimi's for a while longer before heading home to make Dad's supper.

Once Cindy was in kindergarten and I was in third grade, we rode the school bus in Fort Lauderdale together and went to our neighborhood school, but we still saw Mimi weekly. She was a big part of our lives.

> *Mimi was so loving and affectionate. She was my number-one favorite person.*

Mimi didn't like to say goodbye. At the end of each visit she'd walk us to the door holding our hands and giving everyone hugs and kisses. Then she'd follow us outside to the car with more hugs and kisses. She was so loving and affectionate. I always felt really close to her and loved her so much. She was my number-one favorite person.

When I was about eleven years old, I spent the night with her. It was just the two of us. After supper Mimi opened the top drawer of her dresser and brought out a stack of old photographs and letters. We huddled together on her bed. She told me about her life as a girl and read some of the letters. Her eyes danced with excitement, making her look decades younger, as she told me about a boy she once loved.

With a faraway look, Mimi grabbed my hand and told me how he'd walk her home from school. One day he asked her to meet him in the cornfield and they kissed. It was strange to think of my grandmother as young and in love.

I stared at the veins in her sixty-year-old hands. We were decades apart and I didn't know the person she was talking about, but I knew I could never forget Mimi or her touch.

A Burdened Childhood

I did what I was told and rarely got in trouble at school. I was usually the teacher's pet and never was called to the principal's office. I wanted to do what was right and I considered myself a "good kid."

My life at home was difficult. My father was given to drinking and bouts of meanness, often passing out on the couch. There was little love to go around from him and especially toward me. Since I was the oldest, he held me to a higher standard and often complained about me. He accused me of not being a good example for my sisters and not helping out enough around the house.

Even the way I breathed was criticized. I'd had asthma since I was two years old, and sometimes I'd inhale deeply and exhale like I was sighing. It helped me catch my breath, but it aggravated Daddy.

"Cut it out!" he'd growl when he heard me breathe loudly. Dad excelled at hateful remarks and was extremely impatient toward me, but the worst was when he would cut his eyes with a horrible "you repulse me" look. I hated when he looked at me that way. I wanted to curl up and hide. To avoid his verbal abuse and harsh remarks, I learned to breathe very quietly and say as little as possible to him. In fact, I tried to become invisible when he was around.

Mostly Dad subjected me to verbal abuse, but there was always the threat of physical abuse if I didn't do what he said. A couple of times as a teen, he made good on his word—pushing me or shoving me up against the wall. Once he even put his hands around my throat, then looked at me as if to say "you're not even worth it" before he let go and walked out of my room.

My mother was intimidated by my father and offered what little protection she could against his abuse. Thankfully my sisters and I were close. After these times, they'd scurry into my room and we'd huddle together, comforting me as we all cried.

I was a good student, but I was also extremely shy and did not make friends easily. I could sit at my school desk for an entire day and never speak to another person. Just because I was quiet, didn't mean other kids didn't talk to me.

In fifth grade, a boy who sat behind me chided me when I raised my hand to answer a question in class.

"You have skeleton arms," he whispered, but he'd said it loud enough for other students to hear.

Although my appearance was criticized, I took it to mean there was something bad about all of me.

I felt my face turn hot as stifled snickers erupted around me. Even though the bully was in the wrong by teasing me, I felt ashamed and embarrassed. I saw myself as an ugly skeleton, literally. I wanted to melt into my desk and disappear.

In sixth grade I was walking down the hall and a couple of boys pointed, teasing me. "Your legs look like sticks!"

Again, laughter erupted from the other kids who'd heard. His words cut deep. Although my physical appearance was criticized, I took it to mean there was something bad about all of me. I was a petite child, though certainly not the smallest person in my grade, and I internalized the mean-spirited comments to validate the abusive words my father heaped on me. *I'm not worthy. There is something very wrong with me. No one likes me or will ever love me.* The laughter of those children would replay in my mind for decades to come.

My asthma flared up often and I would miss days, sometimes weeks, of school at a time. This made it even more difficult to keep the few friends I had. In my mind, I was invisible, overlooked, and insignificant. In my heart, I longed for a best friend, someone I could share everything with, including my secrets, hopes, and dreams, but that was only another of my childhood fantasies.

Drawn to Spiritual Love

During my preschool years, our family didn't attend church regularly. Mom put out a little nativity set at Christmas and told us the story of baby Jesus. We'd go to church on Easter Sunday, wearing new dresses and shoes, but the rest of the year my parents didn't attend or take us to church.

For a while, I went to church with the Browns, a grandparent-like couple who lived down the street. They were involved in the outreach ministry for their church—in fact; Mr. Brown drove the First Baptist Church bus. On Sunday mornings, he and Mrs. Brown would pull up in front of our house in a short yellow school bus. Mom would walk Cindy and me down our long driveway to meet them. We were the first ones on board since the Browns lived on our road.

We'd stop in other neighborhoods and pick up mostly elementary school-aged children—maybe a dozen or so. After Mr. Brown pulled up in front of the church, greeters took us to our Sunday school classrooms.

The second or third week I attended "big" church (not Sunday school); I listened while the choir sang an invitational hymn. The preacher gave an altar call at the end of each service. "If anyone here loves Jesus and wants to give their heart to Him and make Him the Lord of their life, please come forward." I slipped out of the pew and made my way down the aisle of the giant auditorium, all by myself. Looking back, I'm surprised I was brave enough to go forward by myself as a five-year-old. But I wanted to give my heart to Jesus. I didn't want to miss out on the opportunity.

In front of the altar, I met a middle-aged usher wearing a leisure suit.

"Where are your parents?" he asked, curiously. "Whose little girl is this?"

When no one claimed me, he sent me back to my seat, only for me to do it again the next Sunday. This time he took me more seriously. My Sunday school teacher, a woman in her forties with brown hair and a kind smile, walked down the aisle to explain I was a bus rider. She asked me simply if I was ready to have Jesus come into my heart. I said I was. She prayed for me and accompanied me to my seat.

Even at a tender young age, I was drawn to Jesus.

That became my Sunday morning ritual. I would go forward in an attempt to give my heart to Jesus over and over again. Even at a tender young age, I was drawn to Him. I'm sure I didn't understand what that important faith decision meant, but I knew how I felt. I loved Jesus. I wanted His love, and I wanted Him to have my heart. I didn't realize I could stop giving it to Him after the first time.

In Sunday school we were taught a prayer for the forgiveness of sins, and each night before bed I recited it: "Dear God, please forgive me of my sin and come into my heart. Help me to do the right things and not to do the wrong things. In Jesus's name, amen."

Also during this time I became to worry that if I died before I was baptized, I wouldn't get into heaven. I'm not sure how that notion slipped into my mind, but I had a lot of fears as a child. I worried about not getting into heaven almost daily, and it wasn't just because of my love for Jesus. I remember being terrified of going to hell. During the Sunday school hour, people dressed up as characters and acted out skits. Occasionally, someone dressed like the devil would come in. I sat wide-eyed with fear.

As much as I loved God and Jesus, I knew that Satan, evil, and hell were real. From an early age, I had an awareness that evil crouched in the corners, lurking to catch believers off guard. I tried to be as good as possible so that eternal damnation would not be my fate.

Family Faith

When I was in middle school, we began going to church as a family—all of us except for Dad. It was during this time in my life that my mom was going through her own spiritual searching. She was in her late twenties and life was taking its toll. My dad was drinking all the time and coming home drunk after work every day. It wasn't unusual for us to go out to eat at Red Lobster on Friday night. Dad would drink an entire pitcher of beer and refuse to give Mom the keys.

More than once I remember huddling in the back seat with my younger sisters while Mom cried in the front seat and Dad yelled at her.

He'd veer off the road and then jerk the car back in the lane. He'd stop too fast or too slow, almost hitting cars in front of him.

At that time we still lived in South Florida, where there are canals on both sides of the road. Often we'd come upon an accident scene and see bright flashing lights as a car would be pulled from the dark waters. I lived in fear that we were going to end up in one of those canals because of Dad's drunk driving, so I devised a plan. When the car started over the edge of the road, I would roll down my window. I'd pull the sister closest to me out the window, get her to shore, then dive back in for my other sisters. I only hoped Mom would be able to get out safely on her own. To be honest, I didn't care if Dad got out or not. I didn't care if he drowned and I certainly didn't believe he cared about any of us at all.

Mom told Dad that if he continued to drink, she would leave and take us kids with her.

One night Dad came home after work more drunk than usual. He got on my youngest sister's tricycle and started riding it around. Mom yelled at him and told him to stop acting like a fool. He grabbed her by her arms and hurt her. It left bruises. I couldn't believe my eyes as I watched the whole thing.

That night, after he passed out, Mom sat down and wrote a letter. She told him that she couldn't go on this way. If he continued to drink, she would leave and take us kids with her. She left the letter for him to find the next morning. The very next day my dad came home earlier than he ever had and he had not been drinking. They sat down and talked for a long while.

From that day on, Dad's drinking stopped. But his meanness didn't. In some ways he was even more bitter and difficult to get along with when he was sober. At least when he was drinking he'd have playful moments, and eventually pass out on the couch to give everyone a reprieve.

Mom started reading the Bible, searching for help. Aunt Ethel, Mimi's oldest sister, invited us to her church. One Sunday, my mom, my sisters, and I attended Harding Street Church of Christ for the very first time. It was a small building, much smaller than the First Baptist Church, which took up an entire block. My Sunday school class was in a tiny room in the back and consisted of about six other kids my age. The teacher was a kind, older lady. She was very patient with me when I proudly told her I was a Baptist, and we were only visiting.

She asked me questions about what I learned in Sunday school and what songs I knew. I was happy this church had the same Bible stories and many of the same songs. This Sunday school class was very personal. I liked being made to feel special as a visitor, whereas at First Baptist I was easily overlooked and invisible.

It wasn't long before Mom was baptized and we joined Harding Street. Mom, my sisters, and I attended every service—Sunday morning, Sunday evening, and Wednesday night for Bible classes. Sunday mornings before leaving for church, Mom would pick out an outfit for my dad and lay it on the bed, even though he never went with us.

One weekend my parents had gone out of town, so we kids stayed with Mimi. Aunt Ethel picked us up for church and afterward we went out to eat.

"I'll tell you what," said Aunt Ethel as us girls huddled in a booth. "That was a fine sermon this morning!"

"I know! It even made me feel like I wanted to be baptized," I said in agreement before realizing what I was saying.

Aunt Ethel almost fell out of her chair.

"Really? How long have you been thinking about being baptized?"

"For a while now," I answered somberly. "But am I too young?"

"I'm not able to tell you that." Aunt Ethel grabbed my hand and squeezed it. "Let's talk to some people after church tonight."

That evening after the service, Aunt Ethel and I sat in the pew next to the minister as she told him about our conversation earlier in the day.

"Jesus died on the cross to take away your sins," he said to me. "Asking Him to come into your heart is a lifelong commitment and not something to be taken lightly."

I nodded eagerly and told him I was ready.

"But don't you want to wait for your parents to come home before being baptized?" he asked. "Do you think your mom will be upset if she isn't here?"

"I think she'll be happy for me," I replied.

Even though church had ended, many in the congregation lingered and visited long after services. Aunt Ethel and a couple of the ladies helped me get the baptismal robe on. When I stepped into the baptistery, a number of people were there.

"Do you believe that Jesus is the Son of God?" asked the minister.

"Yes, I do," I answered with a big smile.

"I baptize you in Christ in the name of the Father and the Son and the Holy Spirit."

A great burden was instantly lifted. I didn't realize how long I'd been worried that I wouldn't go to heaven if I died before I was baptized.

Afterward, I thought Mom might be mad, but she wasn't.

"I could never be upset at you for doing something this important. In your heart you knew you were ready," Mom said. "There was no need to wait for me to be there. I'm happy for you."

Love of a Family

I met my husband-to-be after our family moved to North Florida. Mike and I were in ninth grade when my boyfriend at the time introduced us because I wanted to get a job as a cashier at the grocery store owned by Mike's parents. Telling people how we met—that my ex-boyfriend introduced us—has humored Mike over the years.

While working together, Mike and I became fast friends, then close friends, and at one point even best friends. We would tell each other everything. I would talk to him about my crushes, and he would talk to me about girls he wanted to date. We were young and being best friends was more about the "important" things in our lives as teenagers. I never talked about my love for Jesus or my dislike for my dad. We also never talked about being romantic with each other. At that time, I don't think either of us saw the other as anything more than a teenage best friend.

While working together, Mike and I became fast friends, then close friends, and at one point even best friends.

After our high school graduation in 1987, Mike left for a Bible college in Cincinnati. I'd gotten a full scholarship to Lake City Community College, which was in town, so I stayed home, went to classes, and worked full time at the grocery store. Mike and I wrote letters and talked on the phone. We'd get together when he was home from school. After college we started hanging out regularly.

One night after work, I asked Mike "the question": "Who will be the most important person in your life after you get married?" I'd come up with it as a high school junior after reading the biblical account of Abraham sending his servant Eliezer to choose a wife for Isaac. The servant didn't want to make a mistake and bring back the wrong bride, so he asked God to help and prayed: "May it be that when I say to a young woman, 'Please let down your jar that I may have a drink,' and she says, 'Drink, and I will water your camels too'—let her be the one you have chosen for your servant Isaac. By this I will know that you have shown kindness to my master" (Genesis 24:14, NIV).

I prayed to God that the man who gave the right answer to the question would be the one He meant for me to marry. Through years of dating, there'd been a couple of guys who wanted to marry me, and I'd asked them the question: "Who will be the most important person in your life after you get married?" Each of them said, "You will be!" That might have sounded like the right answer, but it wasn't and I declined their proposal.

In the winter of 1990, Mike and I went to see the movie *The Hunt for Red October*. As I drove him home, I asked him, "Who will be the most important person in your life after you get married?" I tried to sound casual as I kept my eyes on the road.

Mike was quiet for a moment. "God is the most important, but my wife would be second and then our children," he answered slowly and thoughtfully.

Bingo! My heartbeat quickened. That was the right answer, but I was surprised. I'd never imagined our relationship in a romantic way. From that moment on, I started to view Mike through different eyes. We started dating exclusively and in the summer of 1991 got engaged.

We married in the fall of 1991, when we were both twenty-two. We wanted to have a baby right away but when it didn't happen, we prayed fervently. Two years later our daughter Amanda was born.

Five more years went by and no more babies. We prayed continuously. Amanda prayed for two sisters and wanted one of them to be named Madeline, after the fearless storybook character. Since I hadn't conceived, the door to adoption opened when a Romanian special aired on TV one night.

In July 1999, the adoption was finalized, but not everything was rosy.

The next morning, I researched international adoption and found two little girls—biological sisters—on a waiting list in Romania. One was named Georgiana and the other was Madalina. I took this as a God wink and contacted the agency. In July 1999, the adoption was finalized and we brought them to America. But not everything was rosy.

The girls had been severely neglected. Madalina, two, had been diagnosed with failure to thrive by a Romanian doctor. Georgiana, three, had special needs. They were like wild children with no language at all other than their "orphanage speak"—a mixture of grunts, mumbles, and huffs. They had their days and nights mixed up. Georgiana hid in closets and nibbled on shoes. Madalina wouldn't make eye contact. She was withdrawn into herself. It was terrifying.

We were told by orphanage workers they would pick up on English quickly. They didn't. We were told by doctors they would catch up quickly from their developmental delays. They didn't. The early days were extremely difficult for them and me, but later years were too. Our girls didn't understand appropriate behavior or responses. They lacked boundaries. I was home with them all the time without a break. Georgie and Madalina would wake me up throughout the night. They threw temper tantrums frequently because they couldn't express their needs and wants to us. Those first few years, I felt hopeless and alone. I cried out to God, but He was silent.

Loss and New Life

Mimi suffered from Alzheimer's disease for nearly two decades. At ninety years old and in a nursing facility, my beloved grandmother had gotten to the point where she just wasn't eating or drinking anymore. I visited one day. As I entered her room, the nurse cautioned me, "Don't be upset. She won't know who you are."

I saw Mimi sitting in her wheelchair, gazing out the window. I gulped hard and sat beside her on the bed.

"Hi, Mimi!" I used an exaggerated voice, hoping to cheer up both of us. I took her hand in mine and looked at her face. I couldn't help but feel like there was still something inside her, like she knew me. Mimi's sparkling blue eyes had dulled with the disease, but then, ever so slowly, she reached over and brushed the hair from my forehead.

I was transported back three decades to my childhood. Part of Mimi's mind may have been gone, but that sweet, loving gesture remained. Even if she didn't remember my name, I knew the love she had for me was still there—even the cruelest disease couldn't take that. Her love was eternal.

On September 9, 2001, Mimi passed away. She had suffered for almost two decades and for many years hadn't been the person she once was, but I still felt sadness at the passing of one of the people I'd loved most in my life. I yearned to be in her presence again, holding her hands and feeling the deep love she had for me.

Mike was working more than seventy hours a week at his dad's store and rarely had a day off. When he did, it would be Sunday, and we would then be expected to eat lunch at his parents' house after church. If I asked to stay home so I could have some time to myself, Mike would get angry. I later learned it was because his family was critical of me if I didn't show up. I was suffocating, not knowing what to do for the girls—these children we'd prayed for so fervently. My faith suffered. I became bitter and resentful.

I didn't know what to do for these children we'd prayed for. My faith suffered. I became bitter.

I loved Georgie and Madalina with all my heart, but caring for them was exhausting. The girls were diagnosed with autism, PTSD, and mental handicaps, and Georgie was also diagnosed with Tourette's syndrome. While they attended special education classes and various therapies, I spent time researching programs or treatments that would benefit them and address their needs.

After a couple of years, depression and severe anxiety crept in. I was suffering emotionally and physically. I started seeing a counselor. It took a decade of therapy before I emerged from this dark time. In many ways, I never have.

It took many years of therapies—occupational, speech, and physical—before the girls acclimated and settled into a routine. I quickly learned that routine was their friend. Anything out of the ordinary would throw them off, even if it was something they knew would happen in the future. Once we all learned how to adjust and live together, life became a bit more manageable.

A month after Amanda graduated from high school; I received one of the biggest surprises of my life. Now in my forties, I was pregnant. After more than a decade of hardship, the Lord was going to bless us with the son we had always wanted.

But I was terrified. While I was ecstatic at the prospect of my son's birth, I was also apprehensive about having a high-risk pregnancy. After a few days of worrying, I realized God Himself is the only one who could have orchestrated this pregnancy, since I had not been able to conceive for so long. This child had to be an answered prayer, albeit answered almost two decades later. These next two trimesters were in His hands.

Our son was born without complications in November 2011. We named him Timothy Michael—Timothy because we wanted him to have a biblical name and Michael, after my husband. At forty-three years old, I'd given up the dream to have another child. Thankfully, God hadn't.

A Dream House

Mike and I were living in town, a mile from the grocery, but I was a country girl at heart. I loved animals and nature, so a home in the country was where I yearned to be.

When we'd first gotten married, Mike promised we could move if we found something within five miles of the store. We'd looked for years, but never found the right house.

One day in 2012, Mike and I were driving home from the store and turned down an old country road we rarely took. A picturesque farm-house came into view, and a "For Sale" sign was posted near the road. We'd heard of this homestead that had been in the owner's family for generations, a twenty-six-acre farm with hayfields, bordered on two sides by a thousand-acre forest and abutting the Everglades on the other.

"Stop the car!" I shouted.

I punched in the real estate agent's number right then and there. We toured the property that very same day and made an offer. It was the perfect place in the country, and only four miles from the store.

A few weeks later, we moved in. Timothy was only two months old. Amanda had gone off to college, Georgie was fifteen, and Madalina was fourteen. The girls had settled down and had grown up enough to be responsible for some of the household chores—cooking, cleaning, laundry, but with supervision. I was thrilled to raise them and Timothy in the country with animals, land, and nature.

I was thrilled to raise the girls and Timothy in the country with animals, land, and nature.

We started a cattle business with a half-dozen head of Black Angus. We raised chickens and had horses and two donkeys as pets. After we'd been there several years, we built a party barn for private events.

The quiet country life did wonders for my overwhelmed soul. Scattered around the farm were gigantic live oak trees, many more than one hundred years old. One of my favorites was a big, beautiful granddaddy live oak sprawled near the back of our house. A wooden swing hung from thick ropes attached to a high branch. The girls loved swinging—going really high in the sky—and I did too. I found great solace sitting under that tree in the evenings, watching the sun go down.

My relationship with God had been burdened with so many of life's problems, but for some reason I felt more peaceful when I was near that tree.

An Awful Eye Injury

We'd lived in our farmhouse for a few months when all of us came down with the flu. Because of the girls' special needs, they required as much care as our five-month-old infant. When they threw up, they did it in their sheets and on the floor. And they wanted Mommy 24/7, even though I was sick too.

I was constantly washing sheets and blankets, disinfecting surfaces, and cleaning the floor. I wasn't able to sleep, since everyone needed me so much, so I didn't remove my daily contact lenses for a few days. I would normally take them out every night before I went to bed, but since I never went to bed during that time, I kept them in.

In addition to taking care of sick people, I still had farm chores— tending our chickens, horses, donkeys, and a brood of ducklings. Each day I had to feed them and change the water in their kiddie pool. It was summertime and hot, so they needed fresh, cool water daily.

I was exhausted from all the work I was doing, both inside and outside. One afternoon, as I was dumping out the dirty pool water, some of it splashed up into my eye. I knew this contaminated water was a dangerous health hazard, and I meant to take out the contact lens, flush my eye with clean water, and put a fresh contact in first thing when I went inside. But the chaos of my house distracted me, and I never changed my contacts.

The next day I had a raging infection in my eye. I needed to go to the doctor, but Timothy had a high fever. I had stayed up with him all night, pushing my own pain aside. Early the next morning, I called Mom and asked her to come over to help with the kids so I could sleep. When I finally lay down it was difficult to fall asleep because my eye hurt so much, but once I was asleep, I didn't wake for hours. When I got up I looked in the mirror. My eye was swollen, red, and really painful.

Again, my need to see a doctor moved to the end of the line. We were closing on our former house that afternoon and I couldn't miss the meeting. We'd been making two house payments for more than six months and were anxious to finalize the sale of our old house.

When I couldn't bear the pain or open my eye anymore, I finally visited a doctor. I was diagnosed with an amoeba in my eye. Several times a day, I had to administer powerful eye drops, which stung and burned, to kill any amoeba.

My eye was saved, but my sight was not restored. It was like looking through wrinkled plastic wrap.

It took more than six months for the infection to clear up. My eye was saved, but my sight was not restored. It was like looking through wrinkled plastic wrap. I could see light and shadows but could not focus on any objects. A few years later, in February 2014, I was able to get a corneal transplant. Doctors hoped the transplant would allow me to see better, but even with contact lenses my eyesight is very poor and my peripheral vision is nonexistent in my left eye. Thankfully, with corrective lenses in both eyes, I'm able to drive, even though I'm legally blind in my left eye.

Pandemic Precautions

When the pandemic began in March 2020, Mike and I knew we would have to take extra precautions in order to keep safe. Georgie and Madalina, at risk due to their special needs, were now young adults, so they usually stayed home during the day anyway. I was homeschooling Timothy, so I had little reason to go out. But Mike had to keep working. He wore a mask, social distanced, and put plastic dividers between the cashiers and customers. Then Mike's dad, whom we called Papa, got sick. In those early days of COVID-19, doctors knew little and there were no proven medical treatments. My mother-in-law had died a few years earlier, so Papa really depended on Mike.

Papa had suffered from COPD for years, so when he first got sick, he assumed it was that. He felt so poorly that he called Mike to come over to his house to help him with his breathing treatments on his CPAP machine.

"You just need to stay home, quit going out, and try to feel better," Mike told him.

But Papa didn't listen. The next day he came over to our house and got in the truck with Mike to feed the cows. At dinner that night, Mike told me about it.

"He's coughing really badly, Sharlene. I'm worried."

The next day Mike checked on his dad and he was worse. Mike's sister was with Papa so she called the doctor, then drove him to the emergency room.

Papa tested positive for COVID on October 8, 2020. Days later, Mike and I were tested. We had COVID too. Mike's fever was one day ahead of mine, and our symptoms were similar except Mike also had respiratory issues.

We were told to quarantine for two weeks. The girls stayed in their rooms on one side of the house, and we stayed in ours on the other. Timothy did his best to stay in his room across the hall from us.

That Sunday my symptoms started—a fever over 104 degrees; body aches, like I had been beaten up; and a pounding headache. At any moment my blood pressure would drop, making me feel so dizzy that I thought I would pass out. I tried all the usual remedies, like putting my head between my knees, drinking warm salt water, and using a cold compress on the back of my neck, but nothing helped.

After four days I was past the fever, but the horrible fatigue and body aches lingered. I felt so weak, and the extreme dizziness made me feel like I would collapse without warning.

> *I felt so weak, and the extreme dizziness made me feel like I would collapse without warning.*

But I had to take care of Mike, who was short of breath and had difficulty walking. I set up the nebulizer for him several times a day and into the night, changed out the humidifier a couple of times a day, and gave him lots of vitamins that our doctors had recommended. Every two hours we alternated with Tylenol or ibuprofen for the fever and body aches.

Meanwhile, Papa was having a horrible experience in the over-crowded rural hospital. He texted us every day, saying how understaffed the facility was. "Whatever you do, do not let them put you in the hospital. It's horrible. I'm going to die here. I'm going to die all alone. If you can get better at home, stay there."

So we did. Mom left meals on our front porch and communicated with extended family about how we were doing. Our church family was praying for us, as were other friends and family who we kept apprised of our condition by group texts.

A week into my COVID illness, I lay on our bed after dinner. I'd been feeling very weak and very light-headed. I felt myself slipping away until a thought floated into my mind: *If I'm feeling this bad, Mike could be feeling worse since he has been sicker than me.* I worried that he may have even passed away. I got up from the bed, but when I did, my feet didn't touch the floor.

Light and Shadows

I was standing beside my bed and starting to walk across the hardwood when it suddenly occurred to me that I couldn't feel the floor beneath my feet. I was confused, but I needed to check on Mike, who had been sleeping in the recliner in the den. I continued to move toward our bedroom door.

Over the past few days walking had been difficult for me due to the dizziness and body aches, but strangely, now it was effortless. Stranger still, I no longer felt sick. As I thought about this, a male voice directly behind my right shoulder spoke to my spirit in an authoritative, yet kind voice.

"It's the prayers of the saints holding you up."

I didn't recognize his voice, but I matter-of-factly accepted his comment. In fact, I didn't even turn around to see who said it. I was on a mission to check on my husband, but the words seemed important so I repeated the phrase out loud: "The prayers of the saints are holding me up." Like a mantra, I began saying it over and over.

As I stepped around the corner from my bedroom into the hall, it was as though my right eye peeled back. I was able to see into another dimension. And amazingly, I could now see with my left eye! The blindness I'd struggled with for the last eight years was gone. My peripheral vision was restored; in fact, my eyesight was crystal clear. Perfect.

I was extremely confused. My sight should have been very blurry since I wasn't wearing my contacts or glasses. Yet, I could see!

As I stood in the hallway, I saw what looked like a curtain, or veil, being slowly pulled back from the right to the left side to reveal the most awesome light I'd ever seen. This light was everywhere. In spite of the fact that it was late at night and the house should be dark, everything was illuminated in a glorious golden-white light. It was the most spectacular color! White and gold at the same time, it was clear and iridescent and beautiful, like looking through a dragonfly's wing.

This brilliant light shone over everything, and it was moving, as if it were alive.

This brilliant light shone over everything, and it was moving, as if it were alive. The best way to describe it is like when the sun comes up in the early mornings and there's a tiny bit of mist and you can see the light as it shimmers and moves. But this light was even more mobile. It was like nothing I had ever seen before.

With this light I could see through the entire structure of our house. The walls and the ceiling seemed to evaporate. Across the hallway, I saw our son, Timothy, in his room on his bed reading a book. He was bathed in the white-golden light, but he seemed totally oblivious to it. I looked toward the den and saw Mike sleeping in his recliner. I didn't see the girls because their room was behind me and I never turned in their direction.

Slowly, the exterior walls of the house disappeared. I saw the world outside our home. The night landscape shone in a beautiful bright light that seemingly went on forever. Even though it was nighttime and dark outside, everything as far as my eyes could see was now light and bright.

I was enthralled by this light. Overwhelmed with joy, I couldn't stay in one place. Each time my eyes saw further into this dimension, I became more and more drawn into this radiant, otherworldly place.

Clearly, I was in a mystical or unearthly realm, but I didn't think it was heaven. I'd slipped inside this other place that seemed to exist alongside the reality I'd lived in all my life. Amazingly this spiritual perception hovered right beside my physical earthly one, coexisting together. It was amazing.

The familiar view of my hallway—the taupe-colored walls plastered with family photos, Timothy's doorway, the room diagonally across from ours, the hallway bench, and our antique upright piano that was down the hall and to the left—faded. All that remained were Mike in the den on the recliner and Timothy reading on his bed.

I was aware that I was no longer inside the confines of my flesh and bone.

I felt separated from my physical body and was aware that I was no longer inside the confines of my flesh and bone. In fact, my senses were heightened and it was as if I now had spiritual perception, a divine understanding that I was experiencing something unique. I wasn't exactly sure where I was or how I got here, but I knew I'd been transported to a pure, holy, and perfect space. I felt happy, peaceful, content, and loved. I wanted to stay here forever.

Even though the bright light shone all around, there were still shadows. Where the hallway bench on my left would have been, I stopped at a sight in the darkness. Two gigantic, grotesque creatures were crouched down; they had dark, bumpy skin like a reptile or amphibian. Definitely not human and larger than a normal human man, they had arms, legs, torsos, shoulders, heads, and necks. Their exaggerated faces were pulled forward, mimicking a snout with long, pointed teeth. The gnarled fingers with pointed thick nails looked like giant claws—long enough to scratch and do serious damage.

They were huddled together, as if plotting an evil act. The sight of them repulsed me. I didn't look at them long because they were too revolting, but I saw hatred, loathing, and fear in their faces. Their dark, beady, angry eyes never looked at me directly but were fixed on something, or someone, above and behind me. I had a sense that those beings were there to hurt me or my family. Fear began to press in. But just when I began to feel afraid, I was overcome with the beauty of the light. I intuitively knew that this light was stronger than evil. Nothing could harm me.

Five Angelic Protectors

I followed the creatures' gazes and turned to my right where the walls and the roof of my house should have been. There stood a gigantic being—the likes of which I'd never seen before. At least eight feet tall, he wore a tightly fitted, brownish-bronze helmet over his shoulder-length hair. Much like the color of aged olive wood that had been polished to a shine, the helmet was beautiful.

He wore a matching bronze breastplate with markings or etchings in a design I didn't recognize or understand. It was polished and shiny, reflecting the light. It reminded me of armor worn by a royal guard, and I thought he must be working for a king. At that moment I realized this soldier *was* working for the King. Without being told, I knew this angel belonged to God and was of Jesus's army.

Around him I saw colors I'd never seen before—more vibrant than I knew on earth—that filtered through and flowed through that glorious light. Illuminated by the golden light, the angel resembled a well-built, fit young man, maybe twenty-five years old. I knew he was an angelic protector—a soldier, a warrior.

> *Without being told, I knew this angel belonged to God and was of Jesus's army.*

I saw joy in his face, playfulness. It was as if he knew me. Youthful and strong, he was not a human man, but he resembled one only without strong masculine features. His perfectly symmetrical, dark eyes were oval shaped. His chiseled nose started at a higher point on his face than human noses do and was more in line with his eyes. He had pronounced cheekbones and a small mouth with thin lips. All the features on his oblong face were perfectly proportional to his larger-than-human face.

He looked down at me with concern. His eyes were filled with so much kindness. I had a sense he knew me and understood everything about me. I knew he was there to protect me.

"You're okay," he said. It was more of a statement and less of a question.

I didn't respond right away. I didn't know what to say. *Was I okay?*

"Are you okay?" he asked.

When he asked that question I recognized his voice. It was the one I'd heard behind me when I first entered this place, assuring me by saying, "It's the prayers of the saints holding you up."

"We are making sure you are okay," he said with conviction. His voice was strong like a commander's yet filled with compassion. Even though I heard his words, his mouth didn't move. Communication was different here. He spoke to me through thoughts. When I would have a thought, he immediately understood, and my thoughts answered him.

"I'm okay, but I need to check on Mike," I said in my mind. Even with everything that was happening here in this surreal situation, I was still consumed with worry about my husband.

The angel instantaneously moved and now stood in front of me, with four more warrior angels behind him. All of them looked different, yet at the same time similar, much like soldiers in the armed forces dress and look alike. None had weapons or swords. I didn't see wings, but their forms seemed to be made of light and covered with the light. They radiated humility and kindness. Without fear, anger, or ego, they stood confident and in charge. I knew they were keeping those ugly creatures from hurting me and my family. They didn't even have to look at or speak to the duo crouched in the corner. Merely by their presence these angelic warriors controlled those evil beings—holding them at bay as they hunkered down and snarled, unable to move.

Everything in this realm felt more real, more tangible than anything I'd ever experienced. And not just things you can touch, like tables, chairs, and other physical objects. Love, joy, peace—all my emotions—felt real and tangible, too, as though they were objects I could hold. This is difficult to explain, but there I understood it so perfectly.

The more I saw, the more there was to see. I started looking around. I moved forward, away from the band of angels, and closer to the light. The illumination mesmerized me. It was irresistible. I couldn't stay in one place.

Each time I saw something else, I was drawn to it. I had a sense that no one faulted me for being attracted to everything in this place.

My Heart Family

As I continued looking around I stopped when I saw dozens of beings of light observing me. Most of them stood alone, in single file, but some were in pairs—all perfectly spaced but not evenly spaced in rows. There were maybe fifty or so. I was curious about them.

"These are the saints," my protector angel said.

Somehow he knew what I was seeing and thinking without me saying a word.

"They are your heart family."

Every word he said was precise and perfectly expressed as a thought—clearly stated so there was no mistake in what he communicated. Unlike here on earth, when inflections and interpretations pollute meanings, in this place each intent and word was perfectly and effortlessly communicated and understood.

I had a knowing that these saints knew me. They looked at me with overwhelming love. They were concerned for me. They watched me as if what was unfolding in this place mattered greatly.

The light continued to draw me in. I moved closer to the saints. All different heights, they had the shape of a human with a head and robes that covered their shoulders and torsos, but they were made of light. I didn't notice their legs or feet because their robes reached all the way to the ground. Beneath their robes, where feet or shoes might have been on a human, the glorious light swirled. All of the beings wore a thin, golden crown on their heads, and there was a thin golden sash around each of their waists.

Their long, beautiful white robes looked as if they were made of fine, pure linen. I walked on the left side of the group, coming closer, needing to understand what this fabric could be. I had never seen linen like this before. It looked lightweight and heavy at the same time, and the light was infused in it and through it. I reached out and touched the linen from one of their robes. It actually had weight and texture, even though it wasn't physical. I was surprised it had substance to it because of the way it looked with the light flowing through it. Like the warrior angels, the garb on these saints looked royal. Heavenly.

> *Like the warrior angels, the garb on these saints looked royal. Heavenly.*

I understood these were special people because they were wearing robes that signified they belonged to the King and they dwelled with Him in heaven.

As I continued studying them, a petite young woman approached. A few inches shorter and much younger than I was, she had soft, light brown curls and the most beautiful blue eyes I'd ever seen. She reached out and took my hands into her own. I felt her touch and a familiarity electrified my being.

Mimi? I was confused. This being didn't look like my grandmother did when I knew her on earth, since she was in her fifties when I was born. Yet her touch was unmistakable. As she held my hands, the love I had for her came rushing back, only now it was overwhelming and all-consuming. Then she touched my forehead ever so lightly, just like she had a thousand times before. *Mimi*! I felt so much love.

Other saints looked on, but none approached—no one other than Mimi. Even so, I understood that everyone there knew me and loved me. I felt that they cared greatly about what was happening to me right now. I also understood that what I did on earth and what happened in my house with the creatures and the angels, with my husband and with my family, all mattered to them.

> *I realized that what happens in the physical world matters to those watching in the spiritual realm.*

A wave of comprehension washed over me, that what happens in the physical realm matters to those watching in the spiritual realm. These worlds overlap. I couldn't see into the spiritual realm until my spiritual eyes were opened. I had slipped through the veil to glimpse how these saints watch my human life, even though I can't see them. I matter. What I do and what happens in my life is of great importance to those on the other side. This knowledge didn't scare me, nor did I question it.

Not only were the saints and angels watching, but the ugly creatures were also paying attention to everything that was happening with me. I knew their goal was to harm. Their loathing was unmistakable— they had a look of hatred more vile than I had ever seen or imagined. Thankfully, the angels were there protecting me and my family from any harm these creatures intended.

I glided effortlessly past the rows of the saints, my feet still not touching the floor or ground. I considered lingering to talk to each one or at least looking harder to try to figure out who each one was, but the beautiful light beckoned me.

As my thoughts turned to the light, one of the saints nearby said: "It is Glory." Another said: "It is Heavenly Father." And yet another said: "He is the Father of Glory."

The saints began speaking in unison, yet I heard each thought spoken in my mind clearly and distinctively as they confirmed who this light was. Their love, adoration, and excitement transferred to me with their words that came to me as thoughts: *Heavenly Father is Glory. This Light is Glory. It is Heavenly Father. He is the Father of Glory.*

The Light began to swirl around me and the saints. The Light moved through them, their robes, their heads, and their thin crowns. It was on the angels and their armor. As I walked through that Light, each individual I passed whispered in awe: *Glory. Heavenly Father. The Father of Glory.*

The lack of a pronoun stood out to me. Not "our" Heavenly Father or "my" Heavenly Father—just Heavenly Father. They knew the Father on a more personal level. This realization overwhelmed me. I was filled with Glory in this place. That Glory was God.

This unearthly Light, white-golden and pure, was in everything and everyone. Glowing and iridescent, it was Heavenly Father and it was called Glory. I was able to understand everything there because of this Light, which reached everywhere. The Light was God.

And the Light was alive. It contained intangibles like love, peace, joy, and contentment that were manifest as real and tangible in that realm.

And the biggest and greatest of these was love. There was an abundance of love. There was more love than I had ever experienced or ever knew existed. I was filled up to the brim, overflowing. This love reached everywhere inside my being, my spiritual being, which was more real than my physical one, which didn't cross over to this place with me. This love was the greatest emotion I had ever felt. It reached places deep inside my soul—empty places I had been longing to have filled my entire life.

Now I knew! I knew my emptiness could only be filled with His love—this love that was Heavenly Father. His love completed me. And I never wanted to leave. I wanted to stay here forever. Here in this place, in this Light, in this love. The purest of love. Holiest of love. The love of Heavenly Father. Forevermore He would be Heavenly Father to me. I would not use the pronoun ever again. It was unnecessary. I was in His presence. I felt His love on me without any earthly hindrances or barriers. And it was the best thing that had ever happened to me. It was the greatest experience of my life.

A Hug from Jesus

I do not know how long I was in that Light—it seemed like such a long time, though time was not measured in that realm. I only know it felt like forever, and I wanted it to be forever.

I started to think about Jesus. As I did, I was drawn further into the Light. Gliding, I moved beyond the area where my physical house once stood. I moved beyond my neighborhood. The saints faded from view as I moved more and more into the Light.

I still had a great concern for Mike. That worry never left me, even with everything I was experiencing in this extramundane environment.

Suddenly the landscape changed. I saw nothing but a beautiful sprawling tree, maybe a live oak, in the distance. It seemed to be about a half mile away. I had a compelling desire to go to that tree. I felt that Jesus was there, and I had an overwhelming urge to see and talk to Him.

As soon as I made the decision to go to the tree, I was transported. I didn't step or glide as I had been doing, but in the blink of an eye, I was there in front of this great big tree. It was much bigger in person—almost twice the size of the granddaddy live oaks on our farm.

> *I didn't step or glide as I had been doing; in the blink of an eye, I was there in front of this great big tree.*

I stood in front of this magnificent, ancient tree and watched the Light swirl around. I let it wash over me. I felt the love of Heavenly Father still with me. Moments passed as I basked in the Light and love. Then Jesus appeared, stepping around from the other side of the giant tree. He seemed so much taller than I imagined Him to be, but in no way unapproachable.

I recognized Him immediately. Masculine, yet gentle in appearance, there was so much Light around Him. He had medium-colored skin, wavy brown hair that brushed the top of His shoulders, and a kind, accepting expression on His face. He wore a white, long-sleeved tunic-style robe that reached His feet. On His shoulders were two beautiful sashes that crisscrossed over His chest and went around His waist. One was a soft, yet bright yellow—the prettiest shade I'd ever seen. The other was bright blue, similar to the sky on a cloudless day.

On His feet were sandals in a color similar to the bronze armor the angels wore. It was a beautiful color, and the sandals were so interesting to me that I couldn't help but study them. They didn't appear to be man-made and were made from a type of material I had never seen. They gave the appearance of being royal, given the material and apparent quality. Everything about Jesus was royal, but also very humble and gentle—even friendly. Even so, I felt nervous in His presence.

Unlike the angels and the saints, Jesus appeared like me—in a human form, but with the Light of Glory all around him and reflecting off of Him. He came close to me and sat down on a gigantic boulder in front of the tree. The boulder appeared weathered, and it was flat on the top, like it was a seat made for Him.

> *I had an overwhelming understanding that Jesus saw me as His child.*

Jesus reached out and took my hands in His. My hands were child-size in comparison, and I realized I was child-size compared to Him. Maybe that was why He was so much taller. Even as a fifty-two-year-old adult woman, I was like a child in His presence. In this moment I had an overwhelming understanding and a mystery was revealed: Jesus saw me as a child—His child.

As I looked down at my hands I noticed His. Close to both wrists were large scars with a hole that went all the way through. This startled me because I had always pictured the nails that held Jesus on the cross to be in the middle of His hands. As I was studying His hands, ever so tenderly He spoke to me.

"You are being held captive by strongholds."

His words fell on me like a beautiful waterfall—overwhelming and pure, powerful enough to wash me clean. He spoke to me inside my thoughts, not audibly. His voice was gentle and kind, understanding yet not somber.

Somehow I knew that Jesus knew everything I thought even before I thought it. With the angel and the saints, I had to think words as though they were speech, but it was different with Jesus. Jesus knew everything about me. There were no secrets. And that was fine with me.

"You carry too many burdens. The load is too much for you to bear."

Immediately, I felt silly. The answer to my pain was so simple—to let Jesus carry my burdens. But I didn't understand how to do this.

Embarrassed, I looked down at His feet again. I was too ashamed to meet His gaze. I could feel Him looking at me. I knew He wanted me to look up at Him, but I just couldn't do it.

I started to sob.

Jesus stood and bent close to me. As He reached out His arms I fell into His loving embrace. His arms wrapped around my shoulders and my cheek rested on His chest over His heart. It was the best hug ever.

"It's okay. I will make it all okay," He said.

And I believed Him. There was no untruth in Him. I knew His words were greater than anything that could hurt me—greater than any of my problems and burdens. I wanted Him to continue talking because it was so wonderful, but so many emotions were bubbling up inside my soul, ready to spill out.

I told Him everything—everything that had happened to me in my life from the time I was a girl to what was going on in my life right then with Mike being so sick and Papa being in the hospital and how much I worried about…everything. I had so many fears!

Laying Down My Burdens

After I finished, Jesus spoke. "These burdens are too much for you to handle," He said.

This time I lifted my gaze to meet His eyes. The kindness and compassion were too much for me right then, so I looked back at His feet.

"You are holding on to too much. Your load is too heavy. I never meant for you to bear these burdens." He paused for a moment and then said firmly, "Give them to Me."

"But I don't know how," I tried to explain.

My tears were still falling. Jesus reached out and wiped them away.

"Lay them down. Lay them all down at My feet." His words were stronger this time, more like a command, yet still spoken softly and with great tenderness. Even though we were talking about serious things, His voice was gentle and easygoing, almost playful. It reminded me of times when my children were small and got frustrated when they couldn't do a simple task, like getting their socks on, and came to me, frantic for help.

Even though we were talking about serious things, His voice was gentle and easygoing.

Suddenly I was seeing events and images from my life. There was no time here, at least not like there was on earth, so these events and images were not chronological; rather, everything seemed to happen at once and quickly. I sat down at Jesus's feet as each burdensome event replayed before my eyes, as if it were happening again. All the original emotions came flooding back as I began to relive the painful parts of my life.

I saw the student who made fun of me when I raised my hand in class and he said, "You have skeleton arms!" As I watched the scene with Jesus, I understood that child had made an offhanded comment to me and was joking. As the event replayed, I saw that my arms were tiny, as my frame was petite, but my arm looked nothing like the skeleton bone I had literally envisioned. I looked fine. In fact, I looked perfect. How easily I had believed that lie.

Jesus talked to me about strongholds, that there are bad ones and good ones. Bad ones are the lies I had picked up along my life's journey. Lies I carried around, lies that burdened me from living the life I should be living. They were lies from the deceiver, the true enemy, but would come from people in my life, people whose paths I'd crossed.

I'd held on to these lies for years, decades even. These included being called ugly by kids way back in elementary school. When I was older, I carried around fears and worries about being overweight. I saw myself as an adult and six weeks pregnant. My doctor was picking on me for being a few pounds too heavy and laughed that I better be careful what I ate while pregnant. I realized then that most of my life had been spent worrying about my weight and my appearance. Although I never felt I looked overweight, I remembered believing that I was.

There were the girls, Georgie and Madalina, tiny and helpless in the orphanage, and my family adopting them in Romania and bringing them home. I was full of hope and dreams and excitement in those beautiful early days, but once I experienced their disabilities and understood they were a part of who the girls were, confusion and anger washed over me. I saw myself consumed with the crashing exhaustion of trying to meet their every need. I saw myself frantic, at the end of my rope, holding one child on each hip as I tried to make sense of how to parent humans who acted out and behaved in a way to which I wasn't accustomed.

I saw myself alone, trying to teach and care for and love our adopted daughters—the girls I thought were a gift from God and being so disappointed that the "gift" felt like a burden. My heart so heavy I didn't think I could go on and feeling so guilty with the resentment I felt toward those around me—Mike, his parents, and Mom for leaving me to deal with it alone. And me feeling guilty for admitting disappointment, for allowing hopelessness to creep into my heart, for giving up at times and sinking into despair. For trying to carry it all on my own. For taking my eyes off heaven.

Then I saw hurtful scenes with my father. I had held on to so much anger and resentment about his rejection and abuse. He wasn't there for me and I really wanted a father to love and protect me.

I had overwhelming resentment because he had never tried to repair our relationship or get to know any of his grandkids. He just gave up and left and blamed all of us for everything and we all just let him because it seemed too much to even try. That burden was so difficult to lay down because I had held on to it for so long, but when it fell at Jesus's feet it dropped down as one of the heaviest burdens I had carried, and my heart lifted. And it felt so good to let that one go. I saw my dad as a young man, and I saw him with disappointments and heartbreaks. I didn't just "see" them, I "felt" them, like a great empathy. And I understood why he had been so emotionally unavailable. He was broken too.

There was the disappointment I carried about my corneal transplant and my eyesight. The questions I had about why I wasn't healed completely when it should have been possible. I saw those long days and nights of suffering, my own wilderness, when darkness swirled around me and I had prayed so hard for healing, asking "Why me?"

I had worries that Mike would stop loving me. Fears that we'd lose our livelihood. I saw the anxious thoughts I had while my children played outside, thinking they might get hurt. The nervousness that kept me from driving on the interstate. The hidden sadness that I wasn't good enough to follow my dream to become a writer. The apprehension I felt that people wouldn't like me for who I was if they really knew me.

And last, I saw my fears about the pandemic. I was so afraid that Papa wouldn't get well. That Mike would get sicker, die, and leave me and our children. I worried that I'd never see my daughter Amanda again, since she lived so far away in Washington State.

Jesus and I talked for a long, long time, all the while holding hands. We covered my entire life. Nothing was hidden from Him. One by one, I let go of those burdens. I physically laid each memory at His feet as if it were a weighted blanket. When He spoke to me it was like the greatest lesson I could ever learn. He was teaching me about life, not admonishing me in any way at all. Jesus showed me how I had carried hurtful events around and held on to them for years

> *Jesus and I talked for a long time, all the while holding hands.*

These memories and events I laid at the feet of Jesus became tangible in this realm. My emotional burdens were like concrete items—most mistakes or minor infractions were small and light while intentional sins or life-altering abuses were heavy and larger. The more hurt I held on to, the heavier the burden became. The size and weight were in proportion to how wounded I felt in my spirit.

My burdens began to stack up—piling one on top of another until they were as high as Jesus's head as He sat there on the rock. Childhood fears and disappointments piled up on top of the anger and bitterness I felt toward my dad. Regrets stacked on top of disappointments about our adopted daughters. Everything was mixed up together and in no particular order. They piled up, pictures and images, some of them still moving and playing as I relived them. The pile grew so high that I became distraught.

> *I laid down all my burdens at Jesus's feet. I felt so much lighter. It was a wonderful feeling.*

"It's getting too big!" I cried, worried that it was too much, even for Jesus.

Jesus stopped my worry in its tracks. He said very simply, "Not for Me. Your burdens are not too heavy for Me."

I turned and looked up at Him. He was smiling the most amazing smile I had ever seen.

"I can handle it. Give Me all of your burdens. I want to carry them."

I laid them all down at His feet. I felt so much lighter. It was a wonderful feeling. There was freedom—freedom from the shackles of the strongholds that I had allowed to enter my life. Jesus wanted so much more for me because of His love, because He loved me so.

Jesus accepted me just the way I was. All my failings and mistakes were already healed and forgiven. If I slipped up (and I would), I knew He wasn't going to send me away from Him. He would teach me as He had just done. His lessons were not too heavy. His yoke was easy, and His burden was light (Matthew 11:28–30).

In that moment, I was healed. Gone were my mistakes, embarrassments, and hurts. I needn't be ashamed any longer. I was perfect, right there in that moment—perfect before His presence. Perfect, because of Him.

A Love Like No Other

The truth was that Jesus saw me as beautiful and perfect. And I loved Him more than I ever had before, more than I thought possible. I still couldn't fathom it, but somehow I mattered to Him so much.

Here in this heavenly place, I knew I would follow Him forever, even though I was already His since I first asked Him to come into my heart at five years old as a First Baptist Church bus rider and at twelve when I was baptized at Aunt Ethel's church. This spiritual event, meeting Jesus face-to-face, feeling His overwhelming love, and handing over my burdens filled me like nothing else. I would follow Him everywhere. I would do anything for Him.

Immediately, some of the words from one of my favorite Bible verses popped into my mind: "Where you go I will go, and where you stay I will stay" (Ruth 1:16, NIV).

I belonged with Jesus in heaven. I wanted to stay with Him forever. I was His child, and just as a child would so easily follow someone they adored, I would follow Him.

It was the most amazing experience to feel this much love and acceptance, to be in the presence of Jesus, my King and Heavenly Father, the Father of Glory. I wanted this moment to last forever. I wanted to bask in this Light—a love like I had never known. The love I had been searching for all my life.

Then Jesus brought forth an image. I saw it in my mind, but also in the space in front of me, between me and Jesus. My husband, Mike, was lying in his recliner in the den. I noticed his face was wracked with pain as he coughed deep and hard. I had a knowing that Mike was still very, very sick.

Another image was presented to me, too, this one of Timothy. He looked so small as he read on his bed. I saw Georgie and Madalina in their room.

I didn't want to leave this heavenly place, but how could I leave my family when they needed me?

I didn't want to leave Jesus. I didn't want to leave this heavenly place—this realm where everything was filled with Heavenly Father's light and love. But how could I leave my family when they needed me?

As soon as I had the thought, I looked up at Jesus. The playfulness was gone from His eyes. He knew my thoughts. He knew everything about me.

In an instant Jesus was gone—everything from that spiritual dimension was.

Back in My Bed

I was lying on my bed on top of the covers, in the same position as when I first lay down. I gazed at the window and could see it was still dark outside. There's no clock in our bedroom, so I wasn't exactly sure of the time or how much time had passed. But I was sure I had returned from the other side of the veil, returned from heaven. Back here, everything was shadowy, and the brilliant Light of love no longer surrounded me.

I felt dizzy and weak, as well as confused and disoriented, but I had a strong urge to go into the den and check on Mike. I sat up. My feet touched the floor. I felt every single step I made down the dark hallway, past Timothy's room where he was still sitting on his bed reading a book. I hurried to the light switch and flipped it on. I clung to the opposite wall as I walked by the bench where the creatures had crouched, then past the old piano.

Although I could no longer see through the walls and the glorious Light was gone, I could still feel Jesus's presence. He was with me, even in this place, where there was darkness and shadows, sickness and pain. I didn't know exactly how or why I had slipped through the veil, but I felt like I had been away for a long time, even though once I came back it was as though no time had passed.

Mike was still in the recliner. He was coughing and trying to get comfortable. I walked near him and sat on the couch. I wanted to tell him everything. But I didn't know where to begin or how to put any of it into words. The experience had been overwhelming with events stacked on top of events, as though they'd happened all at once. How would I ever sort out what had just happened to me?

"When I got up off the bed earlier, my feet didn't touch the floor," I said slowly. "It was the prayers of the saints holding me up."

As soon as I said the words, I knew they didn't make sense in this place.

"What are you talking about?" Mike asked.

He was sick and weak and in no mood to listen to something that didn't make sense, but I needed to explain it. I had an urge to share what had happened to me.

"Earlier, I was on the bed, and I felt really bad, like I was going to pass out. I thought I could easily slip away without any effort. But I was worried about you, so I got off the bed to come in here, but my feet didn't touch the floor."

Mike started coughing again. "You've been pretty sick too. People are praying. Tell them to keep praying."

Those words from my near-death experience brought me comfort and hope, even though I was back home.

It was true—so many people were praying. In the early days of COVID, medical professionals didn't know the best treatment and there was no vaccine. Patients were told to go to the ER and then admitted to the COVID floor; many died. Everyone was afraid.

So we prayed. All of our extended family was praying, church members were praying, friends in the community were praying. Those prayers and the prayers of the saints were holding me up. I never forgot those words from my near-death experience. I repeated them to myself over and over. They brought me comfort and hope, even though I was separated from the Light and back home again.

Medical Attention for Mike

The next day, a doctor we know called to check on us. I told him Mike had tested positive for COVID a week ago, and I'd tested positive a day after him. I had no fever, but still suffered from extreme exhaustion and my blood pressure dropping that caused dizziness and weak spells. I explained that Mike's cough was deep, his breathing labored, his fever high, and his inability to walk across the room without me helping him. After we talked in detail, the doctor expressed great concern.

"You need to get him to the emergency room quickly," he said. "Besides COVID, it sounds like he has pneumonia. That's definitely not something we can treat at home."

Since I still had COVID and was supposed to be quarantined, I called Mike's sister to take him to the ER. We hoped he could be hospitalized with his father, but that facility was full, so Mike went to a hospital in a neighboring town. After they left, Papa's words from his texts played in my mind: *Whatever you do, don't let them put you or Mike into the hospital. I'm going to die here. Alone.*

But what choice did I have?

At the ER Mike was diagnosed with double pneumonia. The attending doctor said he was about a week late getting treatment. Mike was treated for COVID with multiple new treatments, including powerful antibiotics, and put on oxygen. But he didn't get better; instead, he kept getting worse.

I didn't text Papa that Mike was in the hospital because he'd been so adamant about Mike not being admitted. Papa was already so upset and anxious. He didn't need to worry about Mike's health too.

Papa continued to go downhill, and I think at some point he just gave up. He passed away on October 19, 2020, after being in the hospital just over a week. Mike spoke to him over the phone right before he died. Papa told Mike he loved him, and they said goodbye.

The morning Papa died, Mike had been in the hospital for three days, and he declined rapidly after that. The doctors were concerned because they kept thinking and hoping that Mike would "turn a corner" and start getting well, but he didn't. Mike FaceTimed me, telling me how miserable he was feeling and that he could feel himself slipping away.

"I thought how easy it would be to just let go," he whispered. "I closed my eyes and was drifting off when I felt someone shake me hard and yell, 'Don't give up! Keep fighting!'

I was drifting off when I felt someone shake me hard. But when I opened my eyes, there was no one in the room.

"But when I opened my eyes there was no one in the room with me. I felt more alert than I had in days. It was as if someone lent me strength," he said. "I had just enough to fight to live."

Mike told me he had requested that I come visit him, and the hospital staff actually made an exception and would allow me to visit.

The next morning I drove to the hospital. I was still very weak and shaky. I had to park in a distant parking garage and walk. I had no idea it would take as much effort as it did. I needed to stop and rest at several points along the way, but I eventually made it to Mike's room on the COVID floor.

I was suited up with so much gear that it was difficult to move. The nurse told me I could not leave Mike's room. Once I did, I could not go back in. So I stayed all day and late into the night. I listened to every doctor who came in. At one point one of them said Mike was supposed to be lying on his stomach because it would open his lungs and he wouldn't struggle so much to breathe. They had told Mike this, but he was still on his back.

Mike didn't recall hearing that information. No one had tried to help him turn over, and he had no strength to do this on his own. But no one wanted to get close to him. The staff stayed in his room for just a few seconds at a time.

I helped him wash up, shave, and change his clothes. Then I helped him onto his stomach. At first he couldn't breathe, and he started to panic, but I talked him through it, comforting him and telling him he needed to be patient and let his lungs open up.

It was only a few minutes of struggling before Mike began to breathe more freely and his oxygen level started increasing. It was well after visitor's hours (even though at this time there were no visitors allowed, especially on the COVID floor) and the staff started hinting for me to leave. I had gone all day without eating or drinking and was feeling very faint and weak. I didn't think I'd be able to make it to my car, so I started to pray.

I didn't know what to do. I thought of some of my church family who lived near the hospital and wondered if they would be willing to pick me up and get me home, but it was still the early days of COVID. I didn't want to put anyone in a possibly infectious situation.

Just then, my oldest daughter, Amanda, called. She and her husband had flown in from Washington State after hearing Papa had died. They'd landed at the Tampa airport, three hours away, and were driving on the interstate, which went right by the hospital.

I told her Mike was showing some improvement and I had to leave.

"I'm feeling so weak right now," I confided, "I don't think I can make it to the parking garage. I don't know what I'm going to do."

"Mom, you won't believe this," said Amanda. "We're almost there. We can pick you up!" I stepped outside the hospital right as they were pulling up.

Processing My Experience

At first when I returned from my time in heaven, I couldn't understand what had happened, what I had experienced. I tried to talk about it, but the words were so insufficient and the people I tried to tell couldn't understand what I meant. I would try to talk about how my feet hadn't touched the floor and how the beauty of the place sparkled as if I had been looking through a dragonfly's wing. But it was confusing and overwhelming to the people I tried to tell and even to me!

My experience consumed my thoughts, every moment of every day and even late into the night.

My experience consumed my thoughts, every moment of every day and even late into the night. I'd wake up in the middle of the night, wondering about it. *What had happened? What had I experienced?*

I saw it all at once, those events stacked on top of one another. I needed to understand it desperately. I needed to know what had happened. I didn't even know that I'd had a near-death experience at this point, but I knew I'd witnessed something amazing and beautiful.

Once I was stronger and Mike was home from the hospital, I started researching online and eventually began to read reports from others who'd experienced events similar to mine. I learned some had what's called a near-death experience, or NDE, and I determined that's what happened to me.

And because of my NDE, I was different, changed. I was desperate to be in that light again. Whenever I would see light streaming from the sun, I would be transported back, wanting to be in Heavenly Father's presence again. I needed His light and I needed to feel that pure love.

Papa's funeral was the week after he died and our family was grieving him, so it was hard to share my NDE. I began to be drawn to sunlight. I started getting up before dawn to watch the sunrise. I would sit outside in the backyard with the big, open sky and watch the light of dawn coming up over the distant live oak trees as it streamed across the sky.

In these early morning moments, I was alone. I poured my heart out to Heavenly Father. I fell to my knees in tears, crying out loud. No one could hear me other than the animals. This quiet time became my ritual, my lifeline. I found connection with Heavenly Father in this place. I felt Jesus come down and sit beside me. I told Him everything that had happened, even though He already knew. Over and over, morning by morning, I'd pour my heart out and beg Him to help me. I was drowning, with grief, with confusion. I didn't know how to go on.

Things that were important to me before became unimportant. I stopped worrying about politics, world events, money; even my writing dreams went away. I was no longer striving for anything earthly. My focus was on heaven, Heavenly Father, and Jesus, my King. I couldn't wait to be in the Light again.

I also started feeling great love for people—love like I had never known before. I wanted to help others, somehow, in some way, even though I didn't know how. I wanted to draw and paint and write just for the beauty of it. I'd create something and take it outside and hold it up to heaven to show Heavenly Father. I wouldn't even show it to anyone else. I was doing it all for Him.

I started seeing His creation so much more vividly too. Behind our house is a giant crepe myrtle tree with enormous white flowers. I would sit under this tree and inhale the aroma of those flowers. As the flowers would fall around me, I'd study the details of the blossoms, and I would praise Heavenly Father for creating those flowers.

I'd study what seemed like hundreds of bees buzzing around this tree. I watched them closely, mesmerized by their intricate features.

> *I knew I was being answered directly by Heavenly Father. And it was amazing.*

My family noticed the changes in me. They realized something must have happened. I had been growing spiritually throughout my life, but it was as though I had taken a gigantic leap with a new perspective. And I wanted them to come with me. I needed my husband to catch up, so I was always talking to him about spiritual things, about what I had seen, about my morning meetings with Jesus under the tree. I would run inside excited every time Heavenly Father would answer me. It started happening almost every morning. I'd pray something earnestly, and I'd open my Bible or turn on spiritual songs and my reply, my answer, would be right there!

At first I thought it was coincidence, and so did Mike, but after a while I began to realize this was no coincidence. I knew I was being answered directly by Heavenly Father. And it was amazing.

Healing Begins

Mike was drowning in grief over losing his dad. He was angry and bitter and sometimes even resentful of my close relationship with Heavenly Father. There were times he was mean and would say hurtful things. He shut himself off from everyone, including me, and our marriage suffered.

One Sunday morning I prayed for him and I was answered so specifically that I ran inside, all excited to tell him. When I couldn't find him, I started telling the children how Heavenly Father had answered me. Mike overheard me from the den and interpreted it as me complaining to the kids about him. We got into a terrible argument about it, and I spent the entire day and night in bed crying, heartbroken.

Early the next morning, I got up well before the sun and headed for the back door. Because of my grief and my tears, my body was depleted and I had no strength. I stepped down to go outside and fell hard. I slammed up against the glass window of the back door, hitting my nose and falling hard on my knees and wrists. It was such a powerful fall that it was as though something, or someone, had pushed me, shoving me into the solid glass back door. My knees were bloody from hitting the tile and my nose was swollen from hitting the glass.

I sat on the floor for a long time. I didn't know if I should call out for help, but who would I call? Mike and I were angry with each other, so I wasn't going to call out to him for help. I decided I'd meet with Heavenly Father anyway, so I got up, hurting and bleeding, and limped outside. I cried so hard that morning, praying to Heavenly Father— praying for Mike, myself, and my family.

It wasn't long before Mike started healing from his grief and we were able to start really talking. He admitted to feeling jealous of my faith and not knowing how to get to where I was spiritually. My pulling him along, trying to force him to catch up with me, had only made it worse. I stopped pushing and became more gentle and patient with him—just like Jesus had been with me.

Making Sense of My Experience

One Sunday morning I had a meltdown during church. For many weeks after my near-death experience I hoped I would find someone there to talk to about what happened, but I never had the opportunity or the nerve. It was such a strange thing to go through—to be so excited to enter for worship and hoping I'd be given the chance to share about my spiritual experience or find a person I felt safe enough to talk with. But I always left without doing so.

That morning I started crying. I just couldn't get up from the pew even after the last song was sung and last prayer was said. Everyone else got up and was leaving, but still I sat there. I couldn't go.

Mike had been sitting on one side of me and my mom was on the other. When Mike left to get me tissues. I tried telling Mom a little of what was going on, but she didn't understand. She made a joke, which felt very insensitive to me. Mike came back with tissues and one of the elders' wives. She sat down beside me. I began telling her a little about my experience, hesitantly at first. She was wonderfully patient and nonjudgmental. She had kind words for me, but I wasn't able to tell her much of it other than the crouching creatures, the angels, and how since then I'd been obsessed with searching for the Light. She suggested I speak with her and her husband at length. We arranged a date.

Weeks later I sat down with her and her husband. I was truly worried about telling them because I wasn't sure how it would be taken by the church I attended. I've never heard anyone ever talk about such things.

They had many questions about my experience, especially about the physical things leading up to it. In the end they advised me to keep it to myself. They worried others could negatively impact me with skepticism or doubts.

I wondered, too, if I was losing my mind since my heavenly experience was so unusual. I had no earthly place to share what had happened and doubts crept in. I decided to start meeting with a therapist and told her about the experience, asking her to look for any signs that I might be losing my mind or that what had happened to me wasn't real, but imagined.

Partway through telling her, I noticed she was crying. She believed everything I said was true. She said she could tell by the way my eyes looked in certain directions, my facial expressions, and my hand gestures. She said with her training she could tell with the inflection of my voice and the way I described things that I had indeed had a spiritual encounter.

They believed the Lord gave me this experience to help prepare me for what I was about to go through.

I also talked to my primary care physician whom I have a good relationship with. She is a Christian and has a strong faith. She also believed that what I had experienced was real.

My therapist and my medical doctor both said the same thing—they believed the Lord gave me this experience to help me or prepare me for what I was about to go through. Of course, the very next day after my experience, Mike had been taken to the ER and then admitted to the hospital.

Changed by the Light of Love

After my NDE, I knew what mattered most—love, the people in my life, and the people in the world whom my path would cross. I knew I was to love everyone.

When I went to work at the store, I had a difficult time doing my usual jobs as the creative merchandiser as well as the chief financial officer. In the months after my NDE, my work suffered, but on the days when I did go into the store to work, I was drawn to others who loved Jesus and they were drawn to me. It was as though we were pulled together like magnets. These were people I'd never met before, people I'd never talked to before. Some would start talking to me about Jesus, about things they were going through. I came alive talking to other believers. I listened to their troubles and offered them compassion and kindness. I felt I was doing something important.

I was drawn to others who loved Jesus and they were drawn to me, like magnets.

Some of the things I was told were heavy to bear, and even though they were not my burdens, I would carry them. I brought them home with me and would be so drained that I would need to go to bed.

Early the next morning, I'd rise up and run outside to my heavenly meeting spot. Here I would unload the burdens and pour out my heart and pray. My lists grew so long that I would often be outside for four hours or more. I started getting up earlier and earlier. One morning when I went outside, it was still dark. There wasn't even a hint of light coming over the horizon. I had arisen early many times before, but this morning when I looked at the clock on my iPad, it was only four a.m. I sat in the darkness, prayed, and listened. I could hear the night creatures moving around, owls in the oaks, armadillos and possums scurrying through the underbrush, the trilling notes of raccoons in the treetops. All of a sudden, everything grew silent. I waited. The first rays of light lit up the eastern sky and a morning bird made its first call. Immediately, my donkey started braying. Roosters were crowing. I looked at the clock and it was exactly six a.m.

That morning, after praying, I turned to my Bible devotional reading, which was from Genesis 1. I laughed when I read verse 5: "and there was evening and there was morning—the first day." I had always assumed that scripture was written that way for poetic reasons—that there was evening and there was morning the first day. I realized I had just experienced that moment when evening changes to morning. Nocturnal creatures go to sleep, then the morning creatures awaken and start singing praises to their Creator.

This was just one more example of how the entire world looked different to me, how I was seeing it through different eyes.

During my NDE, I learned so many things about heaven, Heavenly Father, Jesus, and myself. They loved us first. They created us because of love. We are Their little children. And Jesus will carry all of our burdens.

Through death, I discovered that no one here on this earth could ever give me what I'd longed for. That empty place can only be filled with love from the One who made me—my Creator. His perfect love was the puzzle piece that had been missing. He completed me and I finally felt wholly and completely loved. With the eyes of my soul, I saw His glory. My life forever changed that October night, when night became brighter than the day and the light of His love gave me the happily ever after I'd always craved.

My Life since My Near-Death Experience

Sharlene Spires

It's been very difficult keeping my NDE inside my heart and not talking about it. When I go for too long without talking, writing, or creating art about it, I get sad. I want to shout from the rooftops what I have seen, but I am also afraid to tell people, partly because I struggle with words to describe my experience. But telling people, sharing love with people, is what I came back to do.

Q *How has your NDE changed the way you live?*

A So much in this world no longer appeals to me. I don't have worldly strivings any longer. I crave beauty and creating.

Sometimes when I drive down the road, I'll see light shining in a way that closely resembles the Light in that place—white and golden at the same time, iridescent and sparkly. I pull over and watch it for a little while. At first Mike was concerned and I know this can get old, but now he's beginning to understand.

Q *Did you have a change in your values and beliefs because of your experience?*

A Yes. Things that mattered to me before don't really matter to me now. I used to be worried about finances or big decisions in life, politics, and world events. But I see them through a different filter now. Love is what matters most. "Love one another," Jesus says throughout the New Testament. I am to love others and myself too. Most importantly, I am to love Heavenly Father and Jesus.

Another thing that changed has been my ability to let go of anger and resentment. I can forgive those who hurt me in the past. I even forgave my dad, who died in 2013. I think this was because I laid the burden at Jesus's feet.

Q *You were very moved by the Light in your NDE. How has it continued to affect you?*

A I love that Light, and I still search for it. I like to get up and watch the sun rise as part of my morning meeting with Jesus. I see it streaming through the trees, reflecting off the waters, reminding me of Glory no matter where I am. Sunrises are not as beautiful as that Light of heaven, but it's the closest I've been able to come to it.

If I go more than a few days without seeing the Light, I start feeling sad. I can't wait for the day when I can be in the Light of eternity again.

Q *You remodeled your house after your NDE. Tell us about that.*

A I couldn't stand the walls in the den between Timothy's room and the hallway where I saw the evil creatures. Every time I looked at the bench I could imagine them hunkering under it. So one day shortly after my NDE, I pulled the bench outside by myself and got rid of it. I also hired a contractor to take down the walls that divided the hall from the living area. I needed our home to be filled with light. The area is now open and bright and beautiful. Sometimes I just stand in that space and relive my NDE all over again. It's holy ground for me.

Momentary Eternity

By Leonard "Jay" Martin, as told to Isabella Campolattaro

*For he has rescued us from the dominion of darkness
and brought us into the kingdom of the Son he loves,
in whom we have redemption, the forgiveness of sins.*

Colossians 1:13–14 (NIV)

I was floating gently, nearly motionless in a vast and inky outer space, dotted by a sprinkling of stars and whirling, nameless celestial colors. I could see earth in the distance, a big globe of swirling white clouds, blue oceans, and continents, just like you see when earth is shown from outer space on TV. I knew I was me, but I had no sense of my body or even thoughts registering, really. There was just a deep sense of pure peace and love and connectedness with God and everything…the great "I Am." No time, no temperature, not even a tiny bit of noise. Just infinite, peaceful, gentle, silent space that felt safe. I carry that peace with me to this day.

As I hovered, inert, I became conscious of what looked like a gigantic galaxy off to the left, with wispy streaks of color and light. Later, back on earth in my broken body, I wondered about that galaxy and scoured the internet to find it for several years. I finally did! It was Andromeda

Galaxy, a real place in the heavens, captured forever by the Hubble Telescope. I knew it firsthand because I saw it in person and was sort of one with it.

An unfamiliar, soothing, feminine voice called my name in the dark stillness. "Jay," the voice called. It was a magnetically beckoning tone, calling me forth to what, I did not know.

> *I think I was in a level of heaven, someplace on the way to the beautiful heavenly landscape I've heard of.*

You might think I was wondering where I was or something, but I wasn't. I was oddly accepting. I've since learned that the Bible talks about levels of heaven. I know some other near-death experiencers have found themselves in "outer space," just like I did. Now I think I was in a level of heaven, someplace on the way to the endless miles of beautiful heavenly landscape I've heard of. One thing I knew for sure: It was a far cry from the South Side of Chicago where I was born and raised.

Born on the South Side

I was born Leonard Jay Martin Jr. in the South Side of Chicago, nicknamed Jay by my dad, who was eating a bag of Jays Chips when my mom asked him what to name me. I know people have an idea of the South Side—that it's a violent, crime-ridden part of big-city Chicago. Yet that's only partly true. There are also some affluent areas with historic buildings, museums, colleges, beaches, and so much more. But that's not the part of South Side where I grew up, for certain.

When I was born, my family lived with my grandparents—my dad's parents—in Englewood. I'm not gonna lie. Englewood was a rough place.

Very rough. The kind of place where drug deals happen on your doorstep and people get shot. Truth is, I didn't have to go outside to see addicts and crime. My dad was a drug dealer and a gang member back then.

My siblings and I saw a lot of things a kid shouldn't see. Drug deals, drugs, weapons, and people you wouldn't normally want around your little kid. While Dad was a "hood," a hoodlum in street jargon, a criminal trying to make a life in a hard place, he was also a dad who loved me and our family, and I felt loved. Eventually Dad got straight and clean, after a prison stint when I was a teen.

Grandma's house was a noisy, busy place, even without drug deals and gangsters. All told, I eventually had eight siblings. I was the oldest. At this writing, I'm forty-five and my sibs include my sisters Shy (forty-four) and Tiana (thirty-nine) and brothers Azia (forty-three), Tommy (forty-one), Remy (twenty-nine), twins Robert and Russell (twenty-eight), and Reggie (twenty-seven). A lot of people lived in my grandparents' house, even before all the kids were born. In addition to my mom and dad and my family, there was Uncle Bud, Uncle Alfred, cousins Tasha, Trina, John-John, Mike-Mike, Cousin Chevell (nicknamed Vell), Cousin Leauva, their mom Auntie Vanessa, and assorted other family who came and went over a period of years.

That big red-and-white city house had a long porch along the front with a little front yard and good-sized backyard with an alley out back. There was a giant lot down the street where we kids played often and built clubhouses, forts, and go-karts, and just acted like kids. I loved my family and we were close. I felt safe, even though I was anything but.

Although all kinds of criminal activity were going on in the neighborhood and under my own roof, I didn't really pay any attention to it.

Maybe I was too young or too busy having fun with my cousins. I guess it all seemed normal. Now, of course, it seems nuts. There'd be fights out in the street a lot. Sometimes gunshots. The drama out in the street and inside the house all blurred together.

As a child, I never really understood why there were different gangs and why they fought each other. I remember even as a little kid wondering what they were arguing about. Sometimes the fights would turn into actual shootouts on our block or the next block over. Neighborhood shootouts were a regular thing.

The cops were out in the street and at our house often, like every weekend or every other weekend: making drug busts or questioning Dad, my grandfather, or my uncles about something or another. The police would come busting into Grandma's house, looking for someone or something. They would knock things over, put holes in the wall, searching—for drugs, weapons, money. My grandmother would hush us kids and rush us to the back room until it was over. We'd be cowering, huddled together, terrified. When the cops were done, we'd tiptoe out, and the house would be a mess. Sometimes the drama was my grandpa, laying into my dad and uncles to stop their madness.

Love in the Mayhem

Through all the chaos and crime, my parents still found a way to show us they loved us, that they cared. They provided for us—food, clothes, toys. They told us often how much they loved us, cuddling us on their laps. Even now, my mom talks like that to me, like I'm her sweet little boy. These feelings of love mixed in with violence were normal—I didn't know any different at the time. At some point I was old enough to understand how hard it would be for my dad and his brothers to fly straight. I mean, they could work at McDonald's for five dollars an hour—or sell drugs for hundreds of dollars. I'm not saying this was right or the choice was a good one, but I could understand their decision.

Eventually my mom saw how bad it was getting and she had enough. Guns and drugs on the bed. Dealers with scales weighing and packaging drugs. Mom didn't want us in that kind of environment. She wanted to move us away from Englewood, away from the mayhem, away from Dad. The only place we could move, though, was to the projects. I think Mom was clueless about how much worse the projects would be, easily ten times worse.

Well, my other grandmother—Mom's mama—got wind of that, and she was not having it—no way, no how. She didn't want her grandbabies and her daughter to move to the projects. She bought a house just five blocks but a world away from the other house and moved in with us so we could be together. I love all my family, but after those years with my dad's family, it was good experiencing some peace. It was also a special time getting to know my mother's side of the family. That house was about building family. It was quiet enough that we could connect in a nurturing way. We had nice Sunday dinners and lived a much more normal life. It was a healing time for my mom and three of my siblings who lived there at the time.

> *I love all my family, but after those years with my dad's family, it was good experiencing some peace.*

The Outsider at School

Up until that point, I was in school with my cousins. Even though it was a tough school in a tough neighborhood, I was with my family and my cousins were my friends. But when we moved, I had to transfer to another elementary school. I was about nine. That was hard, being without my cousins. Harder than you can imagine.

I was a quiet type, different than the other kids. I also had mild asthma, and that made me feel a little more vulnerable than other kids. It didn't help that nobody knew me. I was an outsider. They just didn't get me. I got picked on, bullied so badly it made me cry. Given how violent the neighborhood was, you'd think I was beaten up a lot, but I never was. Thank God. Still, the kids taunted me and called me names, even the girls. You'd think that having a dad who was a gun-packing drug dealer would have made me a tough kid, but it didn't. Because I was living with my close-knit family, however crazy it was, I was more sheltered than most of the kids in school.

Plus, I was just a low-key, sensitive kid. Bullies seem to pick up on that. Some other kids had it way worse than me, though. I stayed in close touch with my dad's family and my cousins, and that made the bullying somewhat bearable. Still, I'd come home crying, although I tried to hide it from my mom and grandmother.

Earning Respect

I'll never forget the day things started changing. I was in fifth grade, and my teacher had to leave the room. She asked for a volunteer to write down names of anyone who talked. Nobody raised their hand, so for whatever reason, she called on me. The very minute she stepped out of the room, the other kids went crazy because they thought I wouldn't snitch. But it felt like my chance to get back at my tormentors. There was a thug in our class named Randy. He was getting everyone worked up. I started to write down his name.

He glared at me and grunted, "You better not write down my name."

I stared at him and continued to act like I wasn't writing, but I was.

He grabbed my hand and said, "Three o'clock," as in meet me at three o'clock to fight.

The teacher came back into the room, and I handed her my list.

I was so scared I was shaking. I spent the rest of the school day watching that clock. This was no joke. Randy was a gang member. What was going to happen? He'd beat me to a pulp. I'd never even hit someone. The clock crept on even though I tried to will it to stop. The bell rang. When everyone, including Randy, rushed out of class, I knew they were all going to be out front, waiting to see Randy pummel me. I was the last one out and, honestly, I tried to get out of facing him by trying to leave through the back door, but it was chained. Resigned, I realized I just had to go do it.

This was no joke. Randy was a gang member. What was going to happen? He'd beat me to a pulp.

I walked out the front door, and the kids formed a circle around me. They were taunting me, pushing me toward the center where Randy was waiting. He was in my face, yelling, and I just stood there, psyching myself up to fight back. Suddenly the principal appeared and broke it up. I was so relieved but still terrified. I ran all the way home.

The next day, I tried to get out of going to school. I was still scared, imagining Randy would finish the job. I couldn't come up with an excuse my mom would believe so off I went. I was sweating bullets as I walked into class. Randy caught my eye and walked over. I braced myself for what was to come.

Randy said, "I respect you. You stood up to me." He repeated it: "I respect you."

After that, things got a little bit better, but it was still rough. The bullying continued. Kids talked about my haircut and my clothes. It was awful, and I was always anxious to get back home so I could be with my real friends—my family. I remember going home one day and heading straight to my room to cry. This time my mom realized something was wrong. She came into my room and asked me what was wrong. I finally told her what had been happening at school. I said, "Mom, nobody likes me. Everybody picks on me. I have no friends in school."

Mom said something I remember to this day: "We're your friends, son! Don't worry about it. You just watch as you get older. Friends will come out of the woodwork."

You know, Mom was right. My family got me through those tough school years, all the way through seventh grade. Then it all changed.

Dancing My Way through School

Ever since I was a little kid, I loved, loved, loved to dance. I was always dancing around the house. This was the late eighties, early nineties, the time of break dancing, house dancing, hip-hop. I definitely had some moves. I danced all I could, learning by watching music videos over and over. I'd copy the moves and then put my own spin on them. I'd listen to music like Grandmaster Flash & the Furious Five.

My cousins and I would dance in the street. Word got out that I was
pretty good. It got so people were curious.

I remember one moment in eighth grade so clearly. I was wearing
a baggy, polka-dot shirt, baggy pants, and patent leather shoes with
metal on the toe tip. I also had a high-top fade haircut. Oh yeah, I was
stylin'! I was walking home from school and saw these guys from the
hood in front of my house dancing. My friend Bryant was there, watching. One of the guys started moving toward me—I thought he wanted
to beat me up.

Instead, he said, menacingly close, "I heard you can dance."

"Yeah," I said, shrugging, low-key
and cool.

Bryant piped up to address my dance
rival. "I bet you can't beat my bro."

At that time there was a thing called
dance battles, where you dance compet-
itively in the street, sometimes for fun and sometimes to settle a beef.
So, the guy in the street and I started a dance battle. We were dancing
against each other, and I did good—good enough that everything
changed after that. I'd found a way to belong and to shine.

Bryant and I started dancing together. Before long, we were really
getting acquainted, talking every time we saw each other and dancing—
lots and lots of dancing. We formed a dance group we first called Delta
Phi Kappa (Greek fraternity names were popular back then) and later
we changed it to Future Three. All those Future Three guys from eighth
grade street dancing? They're still my friends to this day: Bryant, Ced,

*We were dancing
against each other, and
I did good. Everything
changed after that.*

Omari, Marcus, Reese, Gary, and Ed. Little did we know then how far dancing would take us!

More than a Creative Outlet

We kept dancing into high school, getting better and better. We were neighbors and friends, and we spent a lot of time together, trying new moves and perfecting our routines. Pretty soon we started doing talent shows at different schools and entering contests around Chicago. Dancing was huge then and I'll bet crime went down because so many teenagers were occupied with dancing. Even some of the hard-core hoodlums were into it. It used to be that if you were a teenager, the gangs would

> *Being a good dancer was definitely a way to earn the respect of the gang members.*

try to recruit you. But in those days, if you danced and were good, they were hands off. In fact, some gang members liked to dance, and they'd even dance with us a bit. Even some gangbangers had dance troupes. Being a good dancer was definitely a way to earn the respect of the gang members.

You know break dancing? That was one of the dances I did well. It all started when I was just eight years old, and I got interested in dance. Someone would roll out a piece of linoleum in the street, and I'd start break dancing. I used to do the move called the windmill, where you lie on your back and spin with your legs in the air like a windmill, but it was too hard on my neck, so I stopped that. My specialty was a move called pop lock. In this dance, you move your arms, legs, and whole body in wave or jerking motions, then kind of ripple into a sudden locked position. If you've ever seen break dancing, then you can picture these familiar and popular moves.

It wasn't just the dancing that changed our world. The music had deep meaning for us too.

Music about Us and for Us

MTV was at its height then, but it played mostly pop and rock music. Hip-hop, rap, and house music hadn't become popular yet. House music, which originated in Chicago's underground club culture, involves DJs overlaying popular disco and dance music with a fast, repetitive beat. It soon spread all over the country and is still popular in dance clubs today.

For us living on the South Side, though, these new trends in music had more meaning. It was the first time we heard people like us talking about our kind of communities, our kinds of challenges, what was going on where we were. I mean, the musicians were people who grew up in neighborhoods like ours, telling stories with music about what was happening in our world and on inner-city streets, and what it felt like to be us. In that sense, the music and the dancing connected us with others all over the country and even with our very selves, and that felt powerful.

Many people don't know that hip-hop and rap originated as a creative outlet for storytelling the reality of lives of young people like me. Yes, some of the lyrics are violent and ugly, but some of life is violent and ugly too. For young Black men growing up in a place where the odds were against us, this storytelling made us feel seen and heard. It was uplifting. Plus, the beat was cool and good for dancing. So that music, and the dancing it inspired, not only helped me and my friends stay out of trouble, but it also motivated us to reach further with our lives. Turns out, we did reach higher and go further than we could ever have imagined.

A Taste of Fame

Pretty soon, Delta Phi Kappa moved beyond dancing at school and in neighborhood talent shows. The first major gig I remember was at the Regal Theater on the South Side. This was a big deal because a lot of famous performers got their start there, including James Brown, Cab Calloway, Nat King Cole, Aretha Franklin, John Coltrane, Whitney Houston, The Jackson 5, Ludacris, Pearl Jam, and more. One of the upsides of doing shows in bigger venues is we got to see and meet other dancers, pick up some new moves, and set the bar higher for ourselves. Some of these dancers were so good they just blew us away, so we'd practice more and go to more talent shows, so we could do better. And we started getting noticed.

We got invited to dance at shows all around the region. For a while, our group was a little fluid. We'd go to a show, then one of us would join another dance group for a spell, then come back to our group. Eventually, we all got back together as the Future Three. We were good. At one point we opened for the late Bernie Mac, a comedian who would eventually become one of the biggest names in comedy. We did a show in Detroit for the Detroit Lions football player Barry Sanders at Belle Isle Park. Then we started doing concerts with regional stars, dancing before their performances. We were traveling the Midwest every weekend. We danced for performers like the Ghetto Boys, Redman, Method Man, and DJ Quick. They were big back then. They were all fifteen years old. For streetwise teens from the bad part of town, this experience was amazing, and we all knew it.

Back in Chicago we were considered one of the best dance groups around. By then we were dancing all over the city—west side, South Side, and north side. One day we heard that the Apollo, the legendary Harlem theater, was holding auditions for a contest in Chicago to compete in a talent show in New York City. We knew our rival group—one we really wanted to beat—would be there. This would be our chance, even though the auditions were the very next day.

The contest included dancers, singers, and comedians. Picture *America's Got Talent*, back in the day. There were hundreds of contestants from all over—Indiana, Michigan, Minnesota, and even farther away. We made the initial cut for the Chicago contest, then became one of dozens of people trying out to make the next cut—and a chance to go to the Apollo. We were confident but not cocky, because there was serious competition at this point.

We took the stage to perform, and we were totally on. The crowd went crazy.

We showed up and showed off. We took the stage to perform, and we were totally on. The crowd went crazy. I'd never felt that way before. After our performance, all the competitors were brought out on stage. We heard the announcement—we'd won an all-expense paid trip to New York City to compete against world-class acts at the legendary Apollo Theater. We couldn't believe it. Just two weeks later, we hopped on a plane on our way to the Big Apple.

None of us had been to New York before, and it's different than Chicago. If you've been to New York City, you know what an impression it makes, with its huge skyscrapers. The Apollo put us up in a hotel and we could see the Statue of Liberty outside our window. You've heard that old saying "pinch me!"? That was how I felt.

We occasionally took the subway, but mostly we walked everywhere, marveling at the sights and sounds of New York City. Even though we were just kids, we joked about there being a bar on every corner and lots of pizza. Boy, did we eat a lot of New York pizza that weekend (and we were from Chicago, deep-dish pizza capital of the US). Saturday night a driver took us to the Apollo in Harlem so we could rehearse on the stage and run through the actual show.

There was a full house the night of the show. The Apollo was buzzing with excitement. We were nervous but totally itching to dance. Steve Harvey was the emcee and super nice and funny with us, making us feel at ease. We got out there and danced great, but just a little sloppier than usual because of nerves, I think. Still, we thought we had a chance—a good chance—to win. But we didn't. A singer who was a local favorite won, and we didn't feel too bad knowing that. Plus, when we got home to Chicago, we were like celebrities because we had danced at the Apollo. I think reaching those heights inspired us to aspire for more and to connect with something bigger than us.

Something…Someone…Bigger

My mom and my great-grandmother—Big Mama—were Baptist and very religious too. They were always trying to get us to go to church. We used to go when we were little because we had to. All the while growing up, Big Mama talked about Jesus. She and Mom prayed a lot and told us to pray too. So I did. I was taught to believe in God and Jesus as well, but I wouldn't say I was a Christian. I can't say I had anything you'd call a relationship with God. That all changed through dance, in a way.

One of my dance friends, Ed, talked about God, Jesus, and the Bible all the time. The rest of us mostly didn't pay him any mind for the longest time. We were just teenagers having fun and trying to get through. But Ed was all Bible all the time. I mean, it was nonstop. He was an evangelist and very forceful about it. He quoted Scripture, talked about Jesus, was always telling us to be clean and fly straight. You know, for a young teen, it was irritating, and we just ignored him.

But around the time of the Apollo experience, something clicked for all of us. I know it did for me. I mean, I knew God. We all did. But we started openly questioning Him and one another as we wondered how our parents, who had prayed so much, were in the hard positions they were in. It was the idea that there was something…someone…bigger who had propelled us out of the life we lived in Englewood.

We all got hooked, and before long we were reading our Bibles and talking about Scripture all the time.

Even though I'd heard some of the same stuff from my grandma all my young life, hearing it from a young Black brother made a difference. I got hooked. We all got hooked and started listening to what Ed had to say. Before long we were reading our Bibles, too, and talking about Scripture *all the time*. I suspect we were bugging others the way Ed had bugged us. We were still dancing, but I feel like we had more passion and zeal because of our faith in God and belief in a greater purpose fueled by Him. I truly believe God set up that timing with the Apollo Theater because not long after, I needed the spiritual support to endure an avalanche of death.

My First Taste of Death

In life, incredible highs are often mixed with or followed by deep, dark lows. Here I was sixteen, and I'd already experienced so much for a young person. I was feeling empowered and positive about my future. The guys and I were a little puffed up from fame. There was a lot of partying in our dance troupe and community.

One day I was at Omari's house next door, drinking lemonade.

In a few moments, I was struggling to breathe. It was terrifying not being able to catch my breath.

Omari wanted me to try St. Ides, which was like a trendy alcoholic drink. At first I said no, but my buddy kept nagging me. Finally I gave in. I was on the small side and the alcohol hit me quickly and hard. We left the house and walked down the street to get something to eat at a neighborhood restaurant. At first I was feeling no pain. The malt drink was having an effect and it felt good—until it didn't.

Suddenly I started to feel kind of weird and breathless. I knew I was having an asthma attack, but this was way worse than the minor ones I'd had in the past. In a few moments, I was struggling to breathe. It was terrifying not being able to catch my breath. I felt like my lungs were squeezing shut. I struggled to speak, to tell my friend I wasn't feeling good. I couldn't get the words out because I was breathless.

I dropped to my knees and somehow grunted, "Call an ambulance."

I remember the paramedics coming, but I drifted off in the ambulance. Apparently I was out of it for some time and ended up on life support because I'd had a severe asthma attack. When I finally came to later that evening, most of my dance troupe friends were surrounding my bed, holding hands and praying for me. My cousin Vell was there, too, crying over me and praying. I think their prayers saved my life!

When I was fully alert, Vell and my whole family were ecstatic. My parents and grandparents were by my side, overjoyed. My brush with death was quickly forgotten until death loomed larger than ever years later. About a week later, I was discharged and the Future Three got back to dancing.

The End of An Era

We kept on dancing and got some amazing gigs, touring around the Midwest. We were all about seventeen and had been at this dancing thing for a while, but it hadn't lost its shine, and we were still dazzled by opportunities. A lot of well-known performers hire local talent when they're on tour, and Usher hired us as an opening act. We came up with a new move that got the crowd going wild. It involved pulling down our pants and pulling them right back up as we were dancing. Afterward, back in our dressing room, Usher's manager knocked on the door and told us that Usher and his band loved our show and especially the new move. Well, we were bursting with pride then and even more so a year later, when we saw Usher's dancers use it in a video for "You Make Me Wanna."

Those dancing years were great, and we had a few more gigs, but all good things must come to an end, as the saying goes. And they did.

Life…and Death Happens Again

The guys and I were eighteen years old by now. We'd already gradu-ated from high school and like magic, it was time to grow up. One of my buddies got involved with a girl and left the group. Then another. A few of us still danced, but a lot less. I was working for a chain tax firm, a job I'd started part-time way back when I was fifteen. They eventually trained me to prepare taxes and when I was older, the boss encouraged me to go to school to get my CPA. I tried to do that, but eventually quit to make money. So, soon it was no dancing and working part-time doing taxes. I can't lie—I was a little bit lost, not sure what was next, when another brush with death gave me a jolt. I got sick.

> *Grandpa's death and my own health scare reminded me that life is short. I wanted to live.*

I was having severe pain in my side. I felt sick enough that I had to be admitted to the hospital for tests, including biop-sies, blood work, and an MRI. The doc-tors suspected I might have some kind of cancer because they saw something on my MRI. Oddly enough, right then, my maternal grandfather got sick with throat cancer. He was admitted to the very same hospital at the very same time, just a few doors down from me on the cancer ward. The only difference is it turned out I didn't have cancer and got better. The doctors never knew what caused my pain, but they released me after a couple of days when there was nothing conclusive on the tests. Grandpa got worse and died right there in the hospital. His death and my own health scare reminded me that life is short. I wanted to live. With or without dancing, I wanted to live my life. Getting the right girl seemed like an important ingredient to living life.

Looking for Love

I had always been interested in girls. Unlike some of my buddies, though, I wanted true love, not just a fling. Maybe I was more serious than my friends, being kind of an outsider all my life, but I wasn't about to be a player. Anytime I met a girl I liked, I made a point of being a real gentleman, treating her nicely and definitely not cheating. I have to say, a lot of my brothers weren't like that. What's worse, a lot of the girls weren't either. How does the saying go? Nice guys finish last? I seemed to have a knack for meeting girls who played me. I wasn't giving up, though. I was holding out for the real thing. Turns out, love was right around the corner.

A friend of mine was graduating from high school and our crew went to her graduation. Sitting there in the gym, we hooted and hollered when she crossed the stage. Bam! Another young lady crossed the stage after my friend and my heart stopped. Boy, was this girl beautiful! I wanted to meet her. Later, I asked my friend who the girl was. Turns out, the girl would be at the big graduation party later that afternoon. I couldn't wait to meet her. When I arrived, I made a beeline to introduce myself. There was chemistry between us immediately and we couldn't stop talking. I got her number before I left. And the rest, as they say, is history.

Time to Grow Up

I fell hard. She did too. It got so we were spending all our time together, every minute I wasn't working at the tax service office. We'd been together less than a year when my lady got pregnant with our first child. I was twenty and she was nineteen. Our parents were not pleased,

I can tell you that. We weren't ready to get married, so she moved in with my mom and our family well before our baby girl arrived.

When our baby was born, it was love at first sight for me. We named her Hawah, based on Chawah, the Hebrew name Eve, which means "life." Nothing will change your priorities like a child. Dancing on the city scene was dying out for everyone, and it finally fizzled out altogether. By the time we were twenty, our incredible dance journey was totally over. At the time, it didn't matter so much because I was in love with my lady and our new baby Hawah.

My faith and zeal toward religion kind of fizzled. Eventually, God took a back seat.

I wanted to be a good provider, to build a life and future different than my dad's. I started going to school part-time, studying accounting. I also got a job at the Coca-Cola plant, helping with deliveries because my tax office income was commission-based, and I wanted something more reliable. Before too long, I just needed to make money, so I dropped out of school to work full time. We were able to get a little apartment together on the East Side, but making ends meet was a struggle, and eventually we moved back home with Mom and Grandma.

Originally, my lady was pretty interested in my faith. I had been vocal about it and evangelizing to her like I'd been evangelized. Her parents weren't fans of my beliefs. Looking back, I might have been a little overzealous, which might have turned them off. They were staunch, churchgoing Baptists and had very fixed ideas about doctrine. I was crazy about my girlfriend and my baby girl, and it was easier if I didn't argue, even though I didn't agree. Partly as a result, my faith and zeal toward religion kind of fizzled too. Eventually, God took a back seat.

I admit we also didn't stress too much about getting married. I was just focused on making a living and I knew God wouldn't love us any less if we weren't married. As a father and as a family, we were doing so much better than many of my peers. By now I had been promoted at Coca-Cola to merchandiser, meaning I set up displays in the stores. We'd had another baby, Uriyah, which is a Bible name meaning "the light of God." My lady and I got engaged and were looking toward a future together. Later we had a third child on the way. The labor and delivery suite had a window, and just as her head crowned, a rainbow appeared in the sky, so we named her Chana, which means "beautiful and gracious" in Hebrew. Life was good—for a while.

A Big Change of Scenery

There were a lot of changes during those early years together. Love and kids will do that to you. We were still living in the South Side with Mom and Grandma, and it was getting rougher than ever. It looked especially bad through the eyes of an engaged father of three young kids. My fiancé's parents had moved to Columbus, Ohio, where they had family, to get away from the worsening crime. She visited them and decided she liked it and wanted to go, too, but I was holding out. I was a Chi-town boy and didn't want to leave my family or my city. I just couldn't imagine leaving there. Then, something happened to change my mind…and our scenery.

The drug dealers in the South Side had become more and more brazen. As a younger man without kids, it hadn't bothered me much, but it became troubling. If I saw the hoodlums out dealing, me and my guys would go right up to them and tell them to leave. They didn't care, though. They did whatever they wanted. One day we were all out sitting on the stoop at my grandmother's house, talking with friends and neighbors like you do. The kids were all running around playing, like they do anywhere. Something on the ground caught my eye. There on the sidewalk beside my grandmother's house was a bag of crack cocaine. Fear and rage welled up in me. Right then and there I decided we'd move to Columbus. Within a few days, I packed up my Hyundai Accent, my fiancé, and three kids and drove straight through to Ohio. It was 2001. Ironically, that's when my real troubles began.

A Series of Losses

At first, moving seemed hopeful, a fresh start in a safer place. My children's mom and I had been struggling before we moved. I thought things would get better after our move to Ohio. And they did for a little while, but we were young with three young kids. We'd just moved a long way with our bags and our baggage—things were not easy.

We were living in an apartment across the street from my fiancé's parents. I'd stopped going to college at that point so we could get settled and I could provide for my family. I got another job at Coca-Cola, delivering soda. It wasn't what I wanted to do, but I was grateful for the steady income. Even though we were close to her parents where she'd wanted us to be, my fiancé seemed unhappy. Even so, I wasn't willing to give up on us, for the kids' sake and for mine. I loved her, but she didn't seem to care. One day she announced she was breaking up with me, and that was that. What made it worse is that we were broken up but still living under the same roof because we couldn't afford to go out on our own. I was heartbroken.

In the middle of this turmoil with my fiancé, my dad called to tell me my grandma had died. Grandma's home and spirit had been an anchor and shelter for us during those crazy South Side days. I loved her so much and had talked to her on the phone a few times since we'd moved. The last time had been just weeks before. My dad had been living with her after getting out of jail and would give me updates on her health.

Grandma had been sick a lot and was also having memory issues. I could never be sure if she'd remember who I was or what we'd talked about the last time. I'd prepare myself mentally for that possibility every time we talked, but once she heard my voice, she'd perk right up and know it was me. During one of our very last conversations, I'd told her I was coming to see her, which I'd planned to do. Sadly, I didn't make it in time.

I got Dad's call about my grandma dying the same night my fiancé told me she wanted to leave me. It was terrible.

I got Dad's call about my grandma dying the same night my fiancé told me she wanted to leave me. I was feeling some kind of way. It was terrible.

Thank God I was able to go to Grandma's funeral. Even though I was so sad about my lady and my grandma, it was good to see my family and my friends and be in familiar surroundings. We buried Grandma, then I headed home. Right after I got back, my lady said she wanted to get back together. Even though she'd broken my heart, I was overcome with grief and grateful for the comfort of our reconnection. *Now I can grieve properly*, I thought to myself.

Only a few weeks had passed before my fiancé and I were at it again. She wanted to end us again. To make it worse, she couldn't move out right away. We were still under the same roof, but it was clear to me she'd already moved on. I was hurt and angry, trying to grieve Grandma's death and the end of my relationship, parent little kids at home, and work. I was totally overwhelmed. And things got even worse.

About a year later, I got another devastating phone call from my cousin Will. My favorite cousin, Vell, had been shot dead by a gangster on Grandma's lawn. That was the first house I lived in with my parents, siblings, and cousins. It was right there. Vell, who'd prayed over me so fervently years before and celebrated my recovery, was dead. What made it even more shattering was that I had not seen him when I was in Chicago for a short visit only weeks before. He'd called me while I was there, but it had been a very short and busy trip and I just didn't have time. That last time I talked to him, I'd promised he would be the first person I saw when I was back in Chicago. Now it was too late.

I cried out to God, "Why, God?! Why is all this happening?" I prayed all the time, and in this moment of anguish, I couldn't understand. I was totally confused and overwhelmed by all the pain and suffering around me. I pushed down my feelings of despair, fear, and anger. I've since learned you can't run away from your pain because it will catch up to you—one way or another.

Sick and Anxious

As I look back on my life up to that point, I should not have been all that surprised at the turn of events. So much trauma in my childhood, so much violence and despair around us in the South Side, so much pain. It was bound to catch up with me at some point. I wonder now if moving away from the chaos of Chicago to the comparative quiet of Columbus had something to do with the anxiety that started creeping up on me and then turning into a dark cloud that almost swallowed me whole. Maybe in the newfound stillness of suburban living, everything that had been stuffed down deep started to erupt.

If you've ever experienced true anxiety, you know how crippling it is—like a constant buzz of haunting fear that affects your body, mind, and spirit. I'd had it all my life, as a little kid living in the middle of a barrage of danger and chaos, but like I said, it really showed up

> *If you've ever experienced true anxiety, you know how crippling it is—like a constant buzz of haunting fear.*

in the relative quiet of our Columbus life. I soldiered through it for a long time, wanting to provide for my family in our new life. I know now that pushing hard feelings down is poison. I started having such serious anxiety attacks that I'd land in the emergency room, certain I was having a heart attack.

I was barely managing to stay afloat, doing my best to show up for my kids and my job, putting one foot in front of the other. At one point I had to cut back my work hours because of the anxiety and mysterious other symptoms I was having: fatigue, weakness, migraines, and just feeling lousy. Of course, less work meant less money, and then the bills started to pile up—as if everything else wasn't enough to make me anxious. It was a totally vicious stress cycle. After my cousin's death, the grief finally laid me out. I fell into a deep depression, weighed down by sadness, memories, and uncertainty about the future.

After a routine physical in 2005, I was diagnosed with lupus, an autoimmune disease that can contribute to serious anxiety and depression. Major depression is present in approximately 25 percent of lupus patients and major anxiety in 37 percent. While it was good to have an explanation for my mental state as well as the other physical ailments I was experiencing, the diagnosis was just another blow. How much more suffering could I take? After all the chaos and losses, my body was betraying me even though I was still a young man. It seems obvious to me now that this was post-traumatic stress manifesting with a vengeance. I had to find a way to cope, or I wouldn't survive. Thankfully, I did.

Quieting My Mind and Soul

In 2010 I discovered meditation. I read *Autobiography of a Yogi*, a book I found incredibly inspiring and hopeful. It made me think there might be some way for me to manage the ways my mind and body were betraying me. I wanted to be at peace. I admit there were times I wanted to end my life because I was so desperate and hopeless. There is no doubt that meditation saved my life and helped keep me sane. I started out simply, using deep breathing exercises and trying to quiet my mind. Over several months of practice, I learned to sit quietly for fifteen minutes and up to a full hour, both morning and evening. On especially tough days, I would meditate more. This not only quieted my mind and spirit but also drew me closer to God.

> *Meditation not only quieted my mind and spirit but also drew me closer to God.*

I started praying more and saying short prayers all day long, itself a form of meditation. Early on I would pray to God: "Yah, help me understand my path, show me what to do, and guide me in the process."

Though meditation took the edge off, I cannot say I was doing that much better. I simply got to a place where I became used to constant pain. I know that wasn't healthy, but I had to go on. Life had to go on. I had four children who needed their daddy. I had a job to do.

The Hits Keep Coming

It seemed the minute I'd adjusted to a new normal, another axe fell. In 2011, my great-grandma died. The following year, her son died, and the next year, my cousin died from a heart attack while he was sitting in her car. But then a horrible tragedy happened, one that still haunts our family to this day.

In a moment of alcohol-fueled rage, my brother Tommy shot my uncle Craig. Tommy fled on foot and evaded capture, finally turning himself in to the police the next day. That is what can happen to a person who is surrounded by violence and under the influence. (Tommy is in jail in Illinois. I asked him if I could share this difficult event and he told me I could, with the hope that it could help someone turn their life around.) From where I was sitting, it seemed like people I loved were falling like dominoes. I didn't know I was next.

I was thirty-six in 2013. One day I found myself short of breath and just not feeling great. *What could it be now?* I cried out to God. I got myself to the doctor and they ran some tests. They found a pulmonary embolism, which is a blood clot in the artery in the lungs. Untreated it could have killed me. They wanted to put me on blood thinners, and I reluctantly complied. But I didn't like taking medication, so I sought natural ways to dissolve the blood clots. At one point I even stopped taking the medication, confident natural remedies could dissolve the clots. This turned out to be a big mistake, which would dramatically change the course of my life later.

Finding Love amid More Storms

Still, I kept trudging along, trying to be the kind of man I wanted to be, the kind of father my kids needed. Even though my relationship with their mom was tense, I'd always had a good relationship with my kids, who were teenagers by then. They were there for me, and I was there for them. We loved one another more than I can say, with a bond deepened rather than broken by the challenges we'd faced. Even so, I sometimes struggled with loneliness and as a young single man, tried to date, wanting to find someone special to share my life with.

Love does that—gives you a feeling of hope even when the rest of life is stressful.

I'd had a few girlfriends, but none was a keeper for long. A couple broke my heart, which was fragile for sure. I'd just about given up on love when I tried an online dating site. I started communicating with a woman named Cassie, online only at first, then with a few phone calls. We would talk for hours at a time. When we met, there was undeniable chemistry. We started seeing each other regularly. I was cautious, wanting to guard my heart, but I liked this woman.

We'd been dating for seven months when she told me she loved me and wanted to take our relationship to the next level, with mutual commitment. I hadn't heard those three little words in a long time, and it felt good, comforting, and hopeful. Love does that, you know—gives you a feeling of hope even when the rest of life is stressful. I wondered if this was an early sign that my life was finally turning around.

Just when I started to get comfy, I got another piece of bad news. I'd been having some mild chest pain and the doctor checked me out. He explained that I had angina, chest pain caused by reduced blood flow to the heart.

"Don't worry about it," he assured me. He told me I would be okay if I took it easy and worried less. Easier said than done! Here I was, thirty-nine years old with lupus, anxiety, depression, pulmonary blood clots, and now angina. *What's up with this, God? Can't I get a break?*

To make matters worse, my children's mom and I had ongoing conflict and fought over the kids all the time, which not only affected our kids, but also deeply affected me. She would even get physically violent toward me. You'd think that having grown up where and how I did, I could handle it, but it was just the opposite.

Everything changed on August 17, 2016. It was about ten o'clock and I'd just gotten home from work. Normally I'd chill out for a while, return some phone calls, and have a little something to eat. But I wasn't that hungry because I wasn't feeling that hot. I was having chest pains again, but I just wrote it off to angina, brought on by the chronic stress I lived with.

Something prompted me to call my mom and then my friend Malahk. I vaguely remember talking to them and then…nothing. I didn't remember a single thing until I came to two weeks later. The doctors and staff told me I'd walked into the emergency room at Doctor's Hospital and collapsed in front of the check-in desk. I've since come to believe an angel guided me and my car that three-mile drive from my apartment to the hospital because I coded, right then and there, in the ER.

I'm told the ER team sprang into action, and doctors soon determined I'd had a heart attack. They immediately performed an angioscopy—when they inserted a tube in a groin artery to look for blood clots, and in my case, to insert a stent. This stabilized me long enough to send me to a trauma hospital, because my situation was that bad. I was taken by Life Flight medical helicopter to Riverside Hospital, where I coded again twice. Later, I learned they said at the time that I was "the sickest person in Ohio." Meanwhile, someone riffled through my wallet and phone and started contacting my family to let them know of my condition.

One of the first people they called was my sister Shy, who was completely shocked by the sudden news of my dire condition—that I'd coded two or three times again as they were trying to stabilize me. They told her I was in the intensive care unit (ICU), warned her I might not make it, and let her know that loved ones should come see me before it was too late.

They told her I was in the intensive care unit and warned her I might not make it.

"But we're in Chicago!" my sister screamed in a panic.

My mom was in the next room, and upon hearing Shy's scream, was overcome with emotion.

"Not Jay!" Mom apparently cried. "We have to go to Columbus!"

They called my brother Azia, who drove into the city from the Chicago suburbs. Soon, several family members had assembled at Mom's house. My sister stayed at home with her little kids while Mom grabbed some clothes and loaded into the car for the breakneck, pan-icked drive to my bedside in Columbus, five hours away. Less than an hour after they left, the hospital called my sister back.

"I'm sorry, it's too late. He's gone."

"No!" my sister cried out. In despair, she quickly called my mother's cell phone.

Mama, full of faith, said, "The devil is a liar," refusing to believe the hospital's recent report. Bad news travels fast, so soon everyone was learning of my "death" as it spread through social media and cell phones. As soon as he and my other kids learned of my state, my son called Cassie. Shockingly, she had just gotten home from work at the very same hospital, but she turned right back around to rush back to the hospital.

In Transit

While my family was in transit to the hospital, I was in transit somewhere else entirely. I found myself in an amber tunnel, gliding along gently as people reached out to me. They weren't pushing and pulling at me but rather reaching out lovingly. I couldn't see any faces or even if the people were wearing clothes, but I was aware that there were all different kinds of people—different races, ages, sizes.

The people faded from view and the tunnel shifted to something more like a dark highway. There weren't cars or anything, but it had the feeling of a broad highway-type road lined with shrubs. Suddenly the gloomy road and greenery fell away, and I found myself free-floating in the inky darkness of space. Planet Earth was below me, and it looked just like the images we see of earth from space. However, I could discern a tree-shaped glow of energy around the planet.

Off to my left was something like a black hole, but more like a funnel of light, with energy flowing around, just like a vortex. It was swirling slowly, like it wasn't moving at all. If you see pictures of galaxies, it's just like that. The galaxy of vivid colors was off in the distance. It was a very surreal experience. *Is that where I'm going? Is that the way to heaven? Is this the tunnel of light everyone talks about?*

I wasn't afraid, worried, or the least bit troubled. I was serene and curious, comforted even, without a care in the world. The sense of God's powerful presence was overwhelming. What came to my conscious mind even then was John 8:58 (NIV): "'Very truly I tell you,' Jesus answered, 'before Abraham was born, I am!'" I felt at one with God as I never had before, even more so than the briefest glimpses during deep meditation. Somehow, even while I knew I was still Jay, I felt powerful oneness with the great I Am.

> *Somehow, even while I knew I was still Jay, I felt powerful oneness with the great I Am.*

Then that soothing ethereal voice called to me once again. "Jay…Jay," it said, at once strong and gentle, drawing me to it.

I looked around, trying to understand where the voice was coming from. Was it coming from the black-hole type vortex off to my left? Or was it emanating from earth, which was glowing with light and energy? I was torn, not knowing which way I should go. Then somehow, I understood that the voice was coming from earth. I wasn't entirely clear what it would mean to respond to its call, but I suddenly knew I wanted to. And so, that's what I did. It wasn't so much a conscious decision, but more like becoming aware of the voice, and I found myself moving toward it.

Back at the Hospital

My family later told me that at this point, all my kids, their mom, and my girlfriend had rushed to the hospital, finding me in the ICU, dead, but still entangled in the usual frightening assortment of life-sustaining tubes and wires. The hospital kept me alive on machines until my mom arrived.

Since my daughter Hawah was next of kin, she was saddled with the decision to pull the plug. I cannot imagine my poor baby having to make such a decision. She was just eighteen at the time and I was her daddy. Even though they'd said I was gone, she told everyone she was convinced I was still in the shell of a broken body and I wasn't ready to go. The doctors told my family that my organs had already shut down, that they couldn't make any promises about the impact of my condition on my brain. Hawah was not giving up, though. They started to pray. My oldest daughter was sure, she said, that God would bring me back to them.

After several hours praying together at my bedside, everyone went home to get some rest and begin to make funeral plans before the final goodbye. The next day, August 19, 2016, just as my family was mustering the courage to trudge back to the hospital, prepared to let me go, they got an unexpected call from the hospital saying they had found a pulse.

My mom literally jumped up and down in excitement, praising God. Everyone was shocked and in awe that for all intents and purposes I'd come back to life. They rushed back to my bedside, where my girlfriend Cassie and sister Shaterria had been all along. I wasn't breathing on my own, but I had a faint pulse. It wasn't much, but it was hope.

As my family streamed into the hospital, full of relief and joy, what seemed like good news quickly turned dark with sobering reality. The doctor told them that even if I recovered, there was a good chance I'd be in a vegetative state. After the initial heart attack, I'd suffered a total of twenty-six strokes, and there was no telling what was left of me. My family had faith that I was still in my broken body, and they resolved to wait for me to awaken, no matter how long it took. Sometime during this long wait for me to return, I believe I was in the great beyond.

My family continued waiting and praying. My mom was at my bedside, gently stroking my arms, my legs, and my head, murmuring encouragement all the while. Then a call came from my nephew Zay back in Chicago.

"You have to stop rubbing his arm!" he said. Zay, who was hundreds of miles away, went on to relay the unexpected message he'd gotten from me—to stop rubbing my arm.

My family had enough faith to believe that I was somehow communicating from the great beyond.

Huh? My family was confused and spooked by Zay's creepy claim. Yet they all had enough faith in something to believe that, just maybe, I was somehow communicating from the great beyond. Even so, they wanted to bring me back by loving me, so Mom kept right on rubbing.

I learned later that I had been placed in an induced coma for nearly a month, to enable my body to rest and recover and to allow my organs to regain full function. Even though I was largely unconscious, it was during this time that I opened my eyes for the first time, drifting in and out of consciousness over the course of a couple of days. The first person I remember seeing was Mom, rubbing me, my girlfriend at her side. More darkness followed, then I woke briefly again and saw my brother Malaak and his wife Yahdna. I recall her telling me to squeeze her fingers, which I did. Another time, I stirred to find my kids standing by.

The doctors later told me they were stunned that my organs and I were recovering so quickly but concluded that my healthy diet, meditation, and absence of smoking and drinking contributed to my extraordinary recovery. So extraordinary, in fact, that they said I'd surely returned from the dead. My friends and family called me Lazarus! I credit their around-the-clock prayers for me to the Most High God.

As I regained full consciousness, I realized I was on a respirator, which is a terrible feeling, but I was surprisingly calm. After it was finally removed, I could breathe on my own, but I couldn't speak because I'd had a tracheostomy earlier. It felt weird not being able to speak. I would move my mouth but nothing came out. When you've been as sick as I was—well, dead—you realize how much you take for granted when you're healthy. Speaking is one gift I no longer take for granted. Another one is Cassie.

The One

The one constant each time I awoke as I was coming out of the coma was Cassie. I sleepily processed that she had been there nonstop from the very start of this ordeal, even though we'd only just started dating seven months before.

Cassie not only sat by my side, but she also stayed on top of the nursing staff, taking notes and making sure everyone was taking good care of me. I must admit I was surprised. After all this drama and sickness and near death she didn't run or say, "This is just too much." *Wow*, I thought to myself. *This is the ultimate form of loyalty. I can't let her get away.* Something told me: *Do it.*

In a quiet moment, still lying broken in my hospital bed, unable to speak, I reached for her hand, gazed into her eyes with tears welling in mine, and mouthed, "Will you marry me?"

Her sweet face broke into a gentle smile, and she said, "Yes," holding my hand tighter. I felt a rush of peace wash over me. Something had shifted in a cosmic way for sure, but also in my heart. Yes! This woman was forever!

The Road to Recovery

The process of getting me back to anything close to normal was underway. One major goal was to nurse my organs back to full function. For one, my kidneys weren't working. That meant dialysis. I was also on all kinds of medications to coax my heart back to health, and I had a vest that contained a defibrillator to jump-start me if my heart stopped again.

I had to relearn everything. Writing, speaking, walking. I'd been dead and then in an induced coma for nearly a month. It was hard work and exhausting, but I still felt the lingering, mystical energy of my time in heavenly space. It helped me persevere and power through with a spring in my step.

Unbelievably, during almost anything they did to me—the poking, prodding, stitches to suture the places where tubes had been in my neck—I would laugh out loud. One time the nurse looked genuinely alarmed and turning to Cassie asked, "Um, is he okay?"

My girl laughed. "Yeah, he laughs when he is in pain."

One day I was half asleep during one of the procedures, and when I opened my eyes, I saw Grandma and Cousin Reese sitting there. They'd driven all the way from Chicago just to see me and make sure I was okay. That was so unlike Grandma, to take big road trips. It made me very happy. We began talking, cracking jokes about everything that had happened, and my amazing returning appetite.

Mom and Cassie never left my side. I was surrounded by my loves for the entire time, God bless them. All that love and support brought me joy and peace, even without the supernatural peace I'd experienced in heavenly space. And you know what's funny? Up until then, five weeks after my heart attack, not once did I even ask what had happened. I was just so peaceful and grateful I was alive that the how and why didn't matter. Eventually people told me, but I didn't ask.

I knew I had dodged a bullet, and I was a changed man with a second chance at life.

When I finally did, I learned that one of those nasty blood clots from my lungs had made its way to the area of my heart called "the widow-maker." Then, as though the widow-maker wasn't lethal enough, I had an initial stroke, and later, lying half dead in the hospital bed, dozens more, eventually totaling twenty-six strokes. Even though it was shocking to realize what I'd been through, it felt surreal. It didn't really dawn on me how dire my circumstance had been. I knew I had truly dodged a bullet, and I was a changed man with a second chance at life.

After two months I finally left the hospital for a skilled nursing facility. It's a good thing I'd been loaded up with love and light, because this is where the going got tough! For one, the place wasn't all that nice, and the staff seemed a bit neglectful. I'd been surrounded by family 24/7 and had constant care around the clock at the hospital, so this was a real change. I guess it lit a fire under me, though, and I needed it.

I was only at that facility for a few weeks. Cassie jumped through all sorts of hoops to get me admitted to the rehab facility affiliated with the hospital, the OhioHealth Rehabilitation Hospital, which was so much better. The staff was very personable, kind, and helpful.

Like a baby, I had to learn to walk, talk, and think clearly again. And like a baby, I'd been reborn. It had been a long labor, this one. Even so, I was a mess. All the things I'd known how to do had vanished. I was as weak and helpless as an infant.

I tapped deep into my heart to get the energy and drive to keep at it. Solving a small problem or doing simple things like buttoning a shirt or brushing my teeth became monumental tasks I had to sort out one tiny step at a time. My body was not my own.

I'd felt love and joy for my friends and family my whole life, but dying brought this love to life.

For one thing, the lower left side of my body had to be totally reconditioned. I was paralyzed from the stroke and overall physical trauma. I dragged my leg around like a useless appendage for a while, trying to command it to cooperate. The nurses were patient yet tough, pushing me to keep at it. My family and friends encouraged me with loving attention and humor, though sometimes also a talking-to. I was also deeply touched that my coworkers from Coca-Cola came to visit. In fact, even my supervisor and the regional manager showed up for me. I was humbled and full of gratitude for their support.

Throughout my recovery process I felt a lot of love, from Cassie and my family to the friends who showed up. Even my therapists worked me hard in a loving kind of way. This amazing feeling of love and joy wasn't new to me. I'd felt it for my friends and family in smaller doses my whole life. But ironically, dying brought this love to life. The heavenly love I'd experienced multiplied by the love from the people at my bedside. The love, peace, and joy I'd felt in heaven had mushroomed.

Reentry to Life at Home

I'd been in the weird time warp of hospital and rehab, and after a few months, it was time for reentry into the real world. I won't lie. I was a little anxious. I'd been in the pit of emotional hell before my heart attack, and it had killed me. I'd been to heaven, and it had revived me. I'd been on the long, hard road of recovery, and it had restored me. Now, I wondered, would I be able to face the world again, without being saddled by the paralyzing anxiety and sadness that had taken me out before? Turns out, my fears were unfounded. Not only was I reborn, but the world was reborn too.

After my discharge, everything felt fresh and new, even unfamiliar. It was as if I were seeing the world for the very first time with the wonder-filled eyes of childlike curiosity. Cars, the sky, buildings…all were strange to me as if I had never seen them before.

This heavenly tune-up of love and light had a downside, however. My sense of feeling pain and heartache was keen. Now, when I turned on the television and saw human suffering, cruelty, violence, and chaos, I was more deeply moved than ever before. If I'd been a sensitive type before dying, I was now supercharged. I've heard it said that the closer you get to God, the more what pains Him pains you. What angers Him angers you. My close encounter with God had sensitized me even more to both love and joy as well as pain and sorrow.

The inevitable question welled up in me. Why did I choose to come back? To follow the voice back to this broken world? Had I been the one to choose to go back, or had I been sent back for a purpose? That would eventually become clear but only after another foray into darkness.

Into Worldly Darkness

In addition to dealing with my heavenly experience, I had to deal with the fragility of my earthly body. I still had little feeling or movement in my left foot. I wore a portable heart monitor with a defibrillator to help keep my heart in check as it grew stronger. I still had a feeding tube in my side and a draining tube from my gallbladder. Although I was leaving the hospital, I still had a lot of recovering to do. Between inpatient and outpatient rehab, my recovery took four years! Only God could enable me to endure.

Between inpatient and outpatient rehab, my recovery took four years!

Before my heart attack I'd been struggling financially, but over the course of many months in the hospital and rehab, my finances completely fell apart. Once home, I still couldn't work. I was on disability, but my medical bills continued to stack up. Soon after getting home, I'd had to start bankruptcy proceedings. I eventually lost my home and job after twenty years. It was a crushing blow.

Mom begged me to come back to Chicago so she could care for me and help me get back on my feet. It was tempting, but I didn't see how I could do it. I still had follow-up care and more procedures at the hospital in Ohio and wanted to try to sort out my finances. Cassie took me in, enabling me to get the aftercare and follow-up I needed with my various doctors. I was also able to see the bankruptcy through, which while painful and stressful, was also a relief, with all the medical and other bills I'd racked up. It was a hardship for her, but she gently and competently nursed me back to health.

Eventually I did travel back to Chicago, where family and friends held a fundraiser for me and my family. This event humbled me and filled my heart with joy. Some of my old dance buddies danced, sang songs they'd written for me, and had a slide show of my recovery. For the first time, I made some public remarks about my heavenly experience. I don't really like being the center of attention, but it did my heart good to be part of this loving evening.

Toward the end of the night, we had a Q&A session about my experience. People wanted to know everything—my illness, my anxiety and depression, that crazy story of the angel driving me to the hospital, the heart attack, my heavenly visit, and my brutal recovery made tolerable through the love and hope delivered by friends, family, and God Himself. It was amazing to share everything that had happened to me, but in the end, I knew it was time for me to go home to Ohio. To what, I didn't know, but God did.

Chasing Peace

I was still using a walker some of the time and was taking a lot of different medications to help keep me going. I had follow-ups with my medical team every two weeks. Eventually, I was able to take off the heart monitor. The feeding tube was removed, and I resumed eating regular food. The gallbladder tube was also removed. I was better, but it felt like I was still living on a knife's edge, uncertain if my heart would fail me. I couldn't work and that weighed on me. Cassie was supportive, but my own pride couldn't bear being a burden.

Oddly, since dying, my sense of time was distorted. Night and day seemed blurred, and my biorhythms were off. I suffered intense insomnia at night. I found I needed more rest whenever I could get it, throughout the day…even if just a few moments. I had awful nightmares about demons attacking me and my family. One time I dreamed I was dead, that I wouldn't wake up. It was terrifying. I tell people I believe for a long time after my experience it was as though I had one foot in the spiritual realm and one in the earthly domain. *What is this now, God?*

After my prayerful, focused effort to rebuild my silent practice, I started to taste the love-filled experience of heaven.

I knew the answer: It was spiritual warfare of the worst kind. Just as I'd come back more sensitive to both joy and suffering, I also seemed more vulnerable to spiritual attack. I knew what I had to do. I resumed my meditation practice with fresh zeal, clearer focus, and a warrior mentality to chase after that heavenly peace with everything in me.

I was beyond grateful to discover that penetrating the veil of the heavenly realm had dramatically enhanced my ability to reclaim that peace I found with meditation. After my prayerful, focused effort to rebuild my silent practice, I started to taste that stillness and love-filled experience of heaven. Hallelujah! At times during my practice, I was even transported to that same sense of oneness with the great I Am. That place of connectedness with God and others. That timeless place of silence where everything was okay, where everything would always be better than okay. In this newly reclaimed slice of heaven, I asked God what He would have me do. He answered.

Helping Others Find Peace

Since then, I've felt an evolving calling to share my story to help others find peace. About a month after the Chicago benefit, I started talking to people more freely about my experience. You'd be surprised how often the subject came up. Whenever I went in for check-ups or follow-ups, the doctors and medical staff would ask questions. I mean, everyone in the OhioHealth network had heard about my death and recovery, so everyone wanted to know details.

This inspired me to share my story even more. I was too sick to work a traditional job that required a daily routine, but I could continue to spread the message of God's love and peace in other ways. I sent letter after letter to literary agents, television executives, and publishers, but no one responded to me. Then, in September 2022, I got my first podcast interview. Since then, I've done five podcasts and one webinar on my heavenly experience. I know my message helps people, and it feels good to me too. After all, I'm doing what God asked me to do.

The other thing I want to do is to create a physical sanctuary space that epitomizes the beauty and relaxation of meditation. Given my financial challenges, I haven't been able to raise the capital to do that yet, but I have created a website that provides resources to people so they can create a sanctuary space in their own homes.

I continue to explore ways to earn money while I wrestle with the ups and downs of my illnesses and ongoing recovery. My hope in this life and the next is firm, and I want to bless others the way I've been blessed. So, as I continue to walk this out, navigating this physical world after my otherworldly experience, I leave you with this:

The LORD bless you and keep you; the LORD make his face shine on you and be gracious to you; the LORD turn his face toward you and give you peace. (Numbers 6:24–26, NIV)

God willing, I will get this thing called life right the second time around.

My Life since My Near-Death Experience

Jay Martin

My life is forever changed, but I wouldn't change what happened to me. Although my health is still fragile, I have a toddler at home. She is a reminder of the joy of seeing the world through the wonder of a child's eyes. My family—Cassie, all my kids, my extended family—and friends are part of my circle of love, a more blissful and complete love that I might not have known if I hadn't gone to heavenly space.

Q *How has your faith grown since your NDE?*

A More prayer and meditation in my daily routine has definitely grown my faith and challenged me to become a better, stronger man. I meditate as much as I can, which is usually twenty minutes to an hour at least twice a day. I've also made a commitment to help others discover the peace and connection with God we can find through meditation in hopes that doing so will help their faith grow too.

Q *How has your NDE helped you process the losses and trauma of your past?*

A After my heavenly field trip, I was really able to let all the trauma of my past go, because now I know for certain that nobody truly dies. It's a great comfort to know that everyone just transitions from this world to the next. My heavenly excursion makes the pain, suffering, and loss in this world more tolerable.

Go Back and Be Happy

By Julie Papievis, as told to Jennifer Grant

Now may the God of hope fill you with all joy
and peace in believing, that you may abound
in hope by the power of the Holy Spirit.

Romans 15:13 (NKJV)

From the outside, I looked like a happy, vibrant twenty-nine-year-old woman. I was blond, fit, and always bursting with energy. A committed athlete, I'd been training for a biathlon for nearly a year. To strangers, my coworkers, and many of my friends and family members, I'm sure I looked like I was thriving.

In his wonderful book *The Little Prince*, author Antoine de Saint-Exupéry's titular character says: "What is essential is invisible to the eyes." And the truth was, behind my glowing skin and get-up-and-go attitude, a whole world of heartache was hiding, not visible to anyone but me.

It was April 1993, and I was nearing the one-year mark since my five-year marriage had ended. The previous twelve months had been excruciatingly hard. I lived alone for the first time in my life, and I felt lonely and isolated in my silent apartment. And I felt tangled in feelings of embarrassment—and even *shame*—about the fact that my marriage had failed.

I also felt adrift spiritually during that year. Earlier in my life, ever since I was a little girl, I'd felt that Jesus was with me, always listening to me and supporting me. I'd been taught by a loving great-aunt and also by my godmother—both Catholic nuns—that Jesus was *always* nearby.

My great-aunt, Sister Thomas, would say, "Jesus is your brother. Just talk to Him like He's your brother." And I grew up doing just that, feeling close to Jesus not only when learning about Him in confirmation class or when I was taking Communion, but also in regular, ordinary moments. Walking to school, staring out the window in class, running around on the playground—I knew He was right there with me. But during that period after my divorce, when I needed His presence, His listening ear, and His loving heart the most, He felt a million miles away.

> *Earlier in my life, ever since I was a little girl, I'd felt that Jesus was with me, listening to me and supporting me.*

"Are You with me, Jesus?" I'd pray, hot tears again streaming down my cheeks. "Just let me know You're here."

In response, I heard nothing but silence. That He felt absent, indeed that I *felt* nothing, caused my Catholic guilt to flare up and my loneliness to deepen.

I managed to white-knuckle it through that hard year. I went to work. I spent time with my parents and older sister, Tammy, shooing away their deeper questions and instead telling them about casual interactions I'd had at the office or about my workout schedule. The race I was preparing for gave me something major to think and talk about. Most of all, I went to the gym.

Physical exercise had become my focus over that year. Looking back, I see that I was running *away* from my past and running *toward* my future. I ran from my troubles, focusing on strengthening my body and getting faster. I had laser focus on the sound of my shoes hitting the pavement or the gym floor or on my bicycle wheels, whirring away as I sped through a training session. Exercise provided me with much-needed diversion as well as fueled me with a hefty release of endorphins every time I worked out. It made me feel like I was in a flow.

> *Looking back, I see that I was running away from my past and running toward my future.*

Fortunately, as that first year after my divorce came to a close, I started to feel a little bit more like myself again. Whether it was residual runner's high or a new sense of resilience—or a combination of the two—I felt keenly aware of what I'd accomplished: I'd survived!

To reward myself for making it through those painful twelve months, I scheduled some time off from work and booked a trip to Cancun, Mexico. I felt I deserved a getaway to commemorate all I'd been through and to kick off a new, fresh start.

Cancun was dreamy, with its white beaches; bright, warm sun after a long, cold, gray Midwestern winter; and friendly encounters with strangers who—sitting beside me on the beach or at the pool—had no idea about my divorce. They just saw a positive, friendly person who was genuinely interested in chatting with them. I'm a people person and enjoy hearing other people's stories. I loved engaging folks in conversation, learning about their lives and the way they spent their days.

I ran while I was there, but I didn't push myself the way I had been doing at home. These were easy, graceful workouts. I indulged in good food and pretty drinks with colorful paper umbrellas, and I felt my body relax. Cancun afforded me real rest.

Of course, a rude awakening awaited me when I got back to work. The first day back after vacation was its own kind of marathon! As a benefits administrator and accounts receivable manager, I had stacks of paperwork to complete and seemingly endless calls to return. After a grueling ten-hour day, it seemed I'd barely made a dent in all I had to do to catch up.

Then, around six o'clock that evening, the phone on my desk rang. I answered and heard Tammy's cheerful voice.

"Welcome back!" she said. "How was Mexico?"

Glancing at the drab office walls, I imagined the lush sandy beaches and glorious sunsets I'd seen.

"Incredible!" I said, sighing deeply. "But now, of course, I'm swamped."

"I can't wait to hear all about your trip," she said. "Why don't you come over for dinner tonight?"

As I balanced the receiver between my shoulder and ear, I tidied a stack of papers on my desk. My pink skin blazed in contrast to the white and gray envelopes and forms.

"I'd love to!" I said. "But I'm *so* sunburned. I need to stop at the mall for moisturizer after work. I could be there by about seven, though."

I looked forward to telling Tammy and her husband, John, about the beauty I'd witnessed in Mexico and, maybe even more importantly, about the new sense of accomplishment I felt after surviving a year on my own after the divorce. It was a relief to know I'd have good news to share for a change. A few minutes later, I picked up my purse, pushed in my chair, and, looking at the pile of papers on my desk, shrugged my shoulders and thought to myself, *Tomorrow I'll get organized. There's always tomorrow.* I clicked off my light and pulled the door closed.

I then ran my quick errand, buying lotion at a department store at the mall. Walking out, I glanced at my watch; it was 6:55 p.m. I realized I'd be a bit late to Tammy and John's, but I knew they wouldn't mind. I took a deep breath. There was no need to rush.

I didn't know, on that ordinary enough evening in May 1993, that my life was about to change forever.

I didn't know when I got into the car that night, sunburned and looking forward to a relaxing night of conversation and dinner with my sister and brother-in-law, that I was about to visit heaven.

I didn't know that the job I'd left that day would no longer define my life, but that I would be given a new purpose.

I got into the car, buckled my seatbelt, and turned on the engine. Pulling out of the mall parking lot, I never saw the car, driven by a speeding, distracted teenage boy, as it flew through the red light, plowing into my white Mazda, almost completely severing my brain stem.

My New Purpose

In his book *The Path to Purpose*, Stanford professor and human development expert William Damon defines "life purpose" as one's ultimate concern. He writes, "[Purpose] is the final answer to the question 'Why?'" Damon and many other scholars and mental health professionals explain that having a sense of purpose guides our decisions, creates meaning, and offers a sense of direction in all aspects of our lives.

Simply put, knowing your "Why?" is the thing that gets you up in the morning, and it's something I've talked to thousands of people about since my accident. I feel an urgency about communicating the importance of having a sense of calling in life. You see, and I'm sorry to report this is true, only about 25 percent of adults in America claim to have a clear sense of purpose, according to a 2018 report in the *New York Times*. What's more, nearly 40 percent of us either feel "neutral" about whether we have a purpose or say we don't have any purpose or calling at all.

Why does this matter? Research tells us that purpose not only makes our lives meaningful, but actually benefits our physical and mental health. Those who know their "ultimate concern," to quote

> *As a Christian, I believe that God has a purpose for each and every person's life.*

Dr. Damon, sleep better, have fewer heart attacks, and even have a lower risk of dementia. Of course, they are also much happier!

As a Christian, I believe that God has a purpose for each and every person's life. We find that message all throughout the Bible, including in Ephesians 2:10 (NKJV), which reads: "For we are His workmanship, created in Christ Jesus for good works, which God prepared beforehand, that we should walk in them."

Regardless of whether or not they are believers, people find their purpose in many different ways. Some witness someone hurting and feel drawn to help: Serving others in need becomes their ultimate concern.

Others find purpose when they dig deep into their passions: Making art, beautifying public spaces, or mentoring others gets them up in the morning. Still others find their purpose after experiencing a major life change or challenge, like I did.

For me, going through a near-death experience (NDE) and healing from a debilitating set of injuries became *my* pathway to purpose. In the years since my recovery, I've spoken to countless people about my experience. I speak to teen drivers about injury prevention and distracted driving, sharing my miraculous and unforgettable story. I teach adults about estate planning, insurance, and other ways we can—and, dare I say, *should*—prepare for unexpected changes in life. I speak at medical schools, sharing my unique perspective on experiencing an almost completely severed brain stem and living to tell about it.

And, most importantly to me, in telling my story, I assure audiences that there is absolutely no reason to fear death because—on the other side of this life as we know it—God's Holy, loving Spirit is waiting to wrap us up in His love.

All to say, after my accident, my *purpose* is sharing my story, and I'm excited you're here, reading along.

A Word to Skeptics

I've been telling my story for nearly thirty years and in many different contexts. I've appeared on network television, my story's been written up in major newspapers, and—most meaningful to me—I've talked in person to thousands of people affected by post-traumatic stress disorder (PTSD), traumatic brain and spinal cord injuries, and more.

When I tell an audience that not only was I *close* to death after a teen-age driver, going fifty miles per hour, ran through a red light and hit my car—and that I *actually died* and then visited heaven—I sometimes see doubts on people's faces. (This, even though one of my neurosurgeons still refers to me as his "dead patient" and, another, his "miracle girl"!)

I don't blame anyone for being skeptical. If I hadn't experienced it myself, I might feel just the same way.

A central rule of neuroscience holds that all human experience arises from the brain, so some people wonder how a person could have any kind of experience when the brain isn't functioning. I get it, but still, an estimated nine million people, just here in the US, have reported experiencing an NDE. Skeptics say NDEs are just biological or psychological events. But those of us who have experienced them, whether we ever even thought about the afterlife prior to our NDE, are quite certain about what we experienced.

> *Those of us who have had an NDE are quite certain about what we experienced.*

People have reported these experiences throughout history and all over the world, and even some of the most secular scientists and brain researchers have had to concede that these experiences are unexplainable. And others in the scientific community (including those who have had positive NDEs themselves) don't try to defend, define, or explain them, but just appreciate the comfort, new insight, and sense of purpose they can bring.

Wherever you fall on the spectrum of belief in NDEs, I warmly invite you into my story. But there's no need to play soft, inspirational music as you read on. No need for you to become a true believer in NDEs.

I just have a story to tell, a true one. What happened to me was real. It was painful. It's a miracle—both that I survived the crash and that my brain stem healed without surgery—and, yes, this story has a happy ending.

But, as you'll learn, mine's not a "happily ever after" tale, and I never gloss over what continues to be difficult for me. Simply put, there was so much damage to my body when I was hit that day that I'll never be the same. Because of the accident, I did not have the chance to have children; I wasn't able to give my parents grandchildren. I'm also much more susceptible to getting sick than most people, and it takes me longer to heal from illness and injuries, both large and small. I have disabilities that are invisible to most people, but ever present.

But mine *is* a story of hope, forgiveness, and determination, and I want to *live* until I die. After experiencing the peace and joy of heaven, I do not fear my eventual death. I don't cling to this life but look with hope and expectancy to the day when I will return to my true home.

My wish for you is that reading this will greatly encourage and empower you in your own life, and that, when you finish reading it, you will have a new (or renewed) assurance that God loves you and is with you always, even in the most difficult of times.

Back to the Accident

As I said, on that perfectly ordinary Monday evening after a perfectly ordinary (if overly busy) day at work after returning from vacation, my car was violently hit by a reckless driver running a red light.

So much for ordinary life. On impact, my brain stem was nearly completely severed. Witnesses tell me my head was lying on my chest, as if it were disconnected from my body. (Only 4 percent of those who have this kind of brain injury survive and, of those who do, most face what's called a short "nonfunctional" life.)

An off-duty paramedic, who happened to be nearby getting his tires fixed, rushed to the scene when he heard the collision. He gently lifted my head, clearing the airway so that oxygen could pass to my brain. This, in itself, was extraordinary as it prevented me from experiencing further brain damage. It was one of many miracles, one of many signs that God was with me.

Moments later, emergency personnel arrived, used the Jaws of Life to rip the car door from its hinges, and rushed me to the closest level 1 trauma center. One of the paramedics would later tell me that, on arriving at the emergency room, I'd

> *Emergency personnel used the Jaws of Life to rip the car door from its hinges and rushed me to a level 1 trauma center.*

already begun "agonal breathing," the body's response to the brain not getting the oxygen it needs to survive and a sign that a person is very near to death. Brain scans showed no brain function at all.

"When we all last saw you," he told me years later, "it looked hopeless."

In the month that followed, I lay in a hospital bed, in a coma, connected to countless wires, tubes, and machines that worked to measure the pressure in my brain, monitor my heart rate, provide me with nutrients, breathe for me, and much more. I was, to everyone who observed me, completely absent and, likely, not long for this world.

But little did the medical staff, my family, and my friends know that, although to them I was essentially life-*less*, I had never felt *more* alive!

A Visit to Heaven

Many people who have had an NDE say they experienced a feeling of peacefulness, saw a bright light, and saw or spoke with other people. Some also say they felt detached from their physical body during their NDE and had a sensation of returning to their body when it ended. I, too, experienced all these things.

I don't recall how I got there, but I found myself awake in heaven, or in a kind of waiting area at its entrance. One of my first experiences there was being aware of the spaciousness of the place and also being awash in beautiful, pure light. Perfect peace.

I was standing in the middle of a large, round area. There was no color, no shadows, just round walls of light. There were no sounds; just utter silence. It was unusual, but I felt completely at ease. I knew I was *exactly* where I was supposed to be. I felt absolutely no fear.

The best way I can describe heaven is to say that it felt like *home*. The way I see it now, heaven is where I came from and where, someday, I'll return. While there, I felt wrapped in comfort, powerfully enveloped by God's love.

After some time—and "time" isn't quite the right word as I felt outside of place and time—I began to feel restless. Turning my head to the left, I saw an intense white light that outlined the walls and floors of what I thought was an adjacent hallway.

A moment later, I'd somehow moved to the opening of the hallway. It looked long and narrow, and I couldn't see where it ended. On each side of the hallway, light streamed up the walls, like an upside-down waterfall. I felt an urgency to move forward, wanting somehow to become part of the light.

I was about to go forward when I sensed the presence of others behind me.

Suddenly, even though I didn't think I'd turned around, the soft, beautiful, wrinkled faces of my two grandmothers—my mom's mother and my dad's—were before me. I glanced behind them to see if they came in from a different entrance, but the space was so vast, I didn't see other ways in. I only saw light.

I knew I was there because I was dead, but I was not afraid. I didn't *feel* dead. As I said earlier, I'd never felt more alive! I had no idea what happened to bring me there and didn't yet remember my accident. I just felt glad I'd come to this beautiful place. Again, I wasn't frightened, but instead felt filled with peace.

I looked at my grandmothers, eager to communicate with them.

It had only been a few months since Gram, my mom's mom, had died. I last saw her at her home on the night she died. And here we were, together again! She and Grandma Sue, my dad's mom, looked healthy and happy. While some people who have had an NDE see loved elders in heaven as their younger selves, my grandmothers appeared the way they did when I'd last seen them. Their kind, lined faces. Their gray hair, styled just as it had been on earth. Grandma Sue placed one hand on Gram's shoulder, and they both smiled at me. What a gift to be with them again!

Even though they looked the same, I knew there was something different about them. I felt aware that, unlike me, they were no longer physical beings, but spiritual ones. And somehow I realized that

> *I knew I was there because I was dead, but I was not afraid. I didn't feel dead.*

although I was in heaven, I still had a physical body elsewhere. And I knew that body of mine was very badly broken.

Somehow, in heaven I moved without intentionally moving myself just as I spoke without using words. With her hand still resting on Gram's shoulder, Grandma Sue smiled at me. I conveyed my thoughts to both of them, speaking but somehow *not* speaking to them.

"You both look great, and you're so healthy!" I said without speaking. "I'm glad you're happy."

More than anything, I wanted to turn toward the river of light and go further into heaven. I motioned them to come toward me. Again, communicating my thoughts without really speaking out loud, I said, "Okay. Come on, girls, let's go!"

> *I lifted my head to look at Gram. A brilliant and intense blue tunnel of light streamed from behind her eyes.*

"You can't follow us," Gram said, her tone both firm and gentle. "You have to go back."

For the first time since I got to heaven, I felt fear. I didn't want to go back. I just couldn't! I swept my right hand across the left side of my body, which was paralyzed, the side that had taken most of the impact of the accident. I pleaded with them.

"But I can't go back," I said, full of despair. "I'm not physically okay!"

I looked down for a moment and then lifted my head to look at Gram. A brilliant and intense blue tunnel of light streamed from behind her eyes. An endless tunnel. This stained-glass blue color made a stark contrast against the whiteness of the area. I couldn't look away from her piercing blue eyes.

As this penetrating light surrounded me, I was shocked by its physical warmth. I felt as if it was gathering me in its arms to comfort me and to reassure me that everything would be okay. I also sensed that if I walked into this blue light, it would lead to eternity. I couldn't stop staring into this light. Somehow I knew it was the presence of the Lord's holiness. It was a gift: pure love and grace. I felt a tangible peace wash through my body, and then Gram spoke to me again.

"Your body will heal," she said, conveying true authority. In that moment I was sure that God would heal my body. I felt the same deep peace I'd felt when I first arrived there. God had sent my grandmothers to me as angelic messengers. Just like angels in the Bible were sent to give God's people confidence, these angels brought me comfort and consolation. I knew then that everything would be okay and that I did not need to be afraid.

With the same brilliant light in her eyes, Gram spoke her last words to me. "Go back and be happy," she said.

I realized that I didn't yet belong here and needed to go back to my life on earth. A wave of trust moved through me. I trusted that God had a reason and purpose for me not to stay with Him in heaven. I felt bathed in hope and in His love.

And then, much to the shock of just about everyone, more than four weeks after the accident, I woke up.

The Identity Thief

When I opened my eyes, initially I couldn't see. I couldn't open my left eye and my right couldn't process the light; it was glaring and unpleasant, nothing like the warm, welcoming light of heaven. I also couldn't hear out of my left ear and became aware that I was drooling.

Where am I? I wondered.

I realized I was alone, and, after a little while, the place came more into focus. A hospital room. A sink. Clock on the wall. A chair. A window with a view of trees outside. Everything was blurry, though, and I was seeing double.

What happened to my perfect 20/20 vision? I asked myself. (Later, I'd learn that light sensitivity as well as blurred and double vision are very common among those who have experienced brain injuries.)

And my body? I thought of the magnetic dolls I'd played with as a little girl. Taking advantage of their removable body parts, I'd purposely put them together incorrectly sometimes for fun, attaching a head on the end of the doll's arm instead of her hand, and so on. I woke up and felt like one of those dolls—disjointed, awkward, and put together all wrong. I couldn't feel my left side.

> *I woke up feeling disjointed, awkward, and put together all wrong.*

As the blurriness lessened a bit, I reached out and found a corded device looped around the bed rail: a call button. Squinting, I located the red button and pressed it. Only seconds later, a nurse ran into my room.

"You're awake!" she cried. Soon three other nurses rushed into the room, talking excitedly. The commotion and their words spun around me.

"What happened?" I managed to force out a few words in a hoarse whisper that didn't sound like my own voice. My throat hurt, and, lifting my right hand to my neck, I felt something different: loose skin, a tube, and a hole in my neck.

Why is there a hole in my neck? I wondered, not yet able to muster the energy to speak again.

"You were in a really bad car accident, Julie," one of the nurses said, her voice gentle and clear. "A teenager ran a red light and hit your car. You're here at a rehabilitation hospital. The doctors took you off the respirator and put a tracheotomy tube in your throat so you could breathe. That's why you feel that bumpy hole there."

As I tried to process what I was being told, she continued. "It's a *miracle* you woke up."

Snippets of what I'd just been told tumbled around in my mind. *Car accident? Tracheotomy tube? A miracle?* Then I suddenly, urgently, thought of my parents.

"Did anyone call my mom and dad?" I asked. My voice made a breathy croaking sound.

"Yes," the nurse replied. "Your parents know. They'll be here soon."

Medical personnel, such as emergency room doctors and nurses, typically ask new patients a few questions in order to assess if they're "alert and oriented." It helps them evaluate patients' cognitive states and abilities. Doctors often try to discern if patients know their own names or the names of significant others, if they know where they are, if they know what year it is, and if they understand why they are there.

Awaiting my parents' arrival, one of the nurses asked me a few basic questions to gauge if I was oriented, but only after I'd inexplicably asked, "How is my yellow Toyota?" (I still have no idea why I asked that question. I've never driven a yellow Toyota in my life!)

"I'm not sure about your car," she said. "But do you remember the date of the accident?"

I shook my head.

"It was on May 10, 1993," she said, following up by asking, "Do you want us to call your husband?"

"No," I replied. "I'm divorced."

"You're right," she answered.

If she already knew that, then why did she ask? I wondered.

"Can you tell me who is the President of the United States?" she asked.

"Nixon?"

I wasn't interested in the incessant quizzing; I had so many questions about the accident, what was going to happen to me, and so much more. It was no fun playing some kind of *Jeopardy!* game with this nurse!

"Bill Clinton is the President," the nurse reported. "But you're right, Nixon was also a US President, decades ago."

I turned away from her. All of this conversation was exhausting. I felt confused and very, very tired.

"Honey, you just rest," she said kindly. "You have an extremely severe brain stem injury. You were in the hospital for about a month and then transferred to us a few weeks ago. You've been here awhile!"

Again, my mind flooded with questions: *Brain stem? What's a brain stem? Been here awhile? Didn't I just get here?* None of it made any sense.

And then, while adjusting my pillow, the nurse spoke the most shocking words of all.

"Julie," she said. "Don't try to get out of bed. You won't be able to stand or walk. You're paralyzed on your left side."

Paralyzed? It was unthinkable. The person I knew myself to be—in good times and bad—was the strong, athletic Julie. Julie who could *run*. Julie who was in training for a biathlon, running five miles five days a week for an entire year and riding my bicycle even more. Julie, happiest when her body was flooded with endorphins. I was toned and strong. There was *no way* I could be paralyzed.

A little while later, left alone in the room again, I pulled myself to a sitting position, determined to prove that nurse wrong. *What could paralyzed feel like?* I wondered. It took a great effort to move at all, but somehow I lowered the rail of my bed and guided my left leg over the side of the bed with my right arm. With both legs dangling over the side of the bed, my hand brushed against something bulky under my thin cotton hospital gown. As the embarrassing realization that I was wearing a diaper hit me, I slid my body off the bed, determined to stand. I ended up in an awkward heap on the floor.

Where was the Julie I knew myself to be?

This person—weak, broken, and actually wearing a *diaper*—couldn't be her. Couldn't be *me*. Like an identity thief, my traumatic brain injury stole my real self, leaving me compromised and illegible, like a bad photocopy. It stole my dreams

Like an identity thief, my traumatic brain injury stole my real self, leaving me compromised and illegible.

and hopes for the future. It erased cherished memories. It left me having to redefine myself, having to start over again to figure out who I was.

One survivor of brain injury, speaking to a researcher at University of Oklahoma's Suicide Prevention Resource Center, described the "identity thief" like this:

"The worst part is, with traumatic brain injury, people can't see it. And they see on the outside that I move around. I do this, and I do that, but they don't see the struggle inside: the memory loss, the struggles to remember, the struggles to forget," he said.

Having now spoken to countless people who have experienced catastrophic injuries, I know the parts of our stories we share. Of course, we are all individuals with particular challenges. I, for instance, don't struggle with memory, but one of the challenges I've lived with is that I don't have a community of others who have survived damage to the brain stem as so very few of us survive.

I know that in order to survive, those of us who have experienced a catastrophic injury need to work toward accepting the new version of who we are. We have to accept reality and we must adjust to what some might call "the new normal" of our lives. For me, as for others who have made this recovery journey, it was a very long, very slow, very incremental process.

> *Those of us who have experienced catastrophic injury need to work toward accepting the new version of who we are.*

Sadly, it's one that not everyone is able to see through to the end. That identity thief sometimes gets the best of people with traumatic brain injury (TBI), and too many take their own lives. One of my doctors explained that survivors of a TBI often commit suicide because they "just can't get over the hump and live with their own perceived sense of failure to meet the expectations of an able-bodied world."

That was the case for a neighbor of mine who lived in the apartment complex I moved to after rehab and after a month's stay at my parents' house. A survivor of a serious brain injury, he took his life by overdosing on drugs. I felt deeply shaken by his choice while, at the same time, I felt such empathy for him.

So often during the first months of my recovery, I'd felt like I was stuck between floors on an elevator: I couldn't go back down to where I was before—Julie the young athlete whose body was strong and invincible—and I couldn't go up to where I wanted to be and to where I knew in my heart that I would be one day—back to the comfort of my heavenly home. I felt stuck.

Despite the depths of depression and emotional turmoil I'd find myself in over the next years of recovery, I knew I could never take my own life. God had given me a second chance and provided countless miracles, even at the scene of my accident, in order that I'd survive. I knew I was meant to be here. So, although I understood the despair that would drive someone with a TBI to suicide, I could never do it myself.

But that day, as the nurses anxiously scrambled to get my broken body back into the hospital bed, I just felt robbed. Afraid, angry, and the victim of an unspeakable wrong. In contrast to the warmth and wholeness I'd experienced in heaven, I simply felt bereft.

When my parents arrived, breathless and thrilled to see me awake, I couldn't find words to tell them what I'd experienced or how I was feeling in that moment. I knew they'd suffered greatly in the month since the accident, sitting by my bedside and praying for me for so long. They looked older to me, aged by their grief and worry. I knew I should feel grateful to be alive, and indeed I was, but it felt complicated. That night I couldn't sleep. I just kept crying. Even more than the shock of facing this new reality, I felt homesick: I was homesick for heaven.

How could God want me to come back for *this*?

I lay in bed and cried my old, familiar prayer: "Are you with me, Jesus? Just let me know you're here."

I know I would have never made it through this time were it not for the memory of heaven and the hope God shared with me through my grandmothers. They had assured me that I would heal. Deep down, I knew it must be true.

Traumatic Brain Injury: The Basics

I have always believed that knowledge is power, so almost from the start after my accident, I delved into learning about the brain stem. Once, early on, I even brought a textbook to an appointment with my doctor, having highlighted several passages that I wanted him to clarify. I was now both a survivor *and* a student of traumatic brain injury.

So while I've become well-versed on TBIs over the past thirty years, I always remind myself that not everyone has had the opportunity to learn about it. I know it can be helpful to educate others, starting with the basics, about what TBI actually is.

Simply put, a TBI is the result of a jolt to the head that disrupts the function of the brain. It's one of the most common causes of disability and death in adults. Every year in the US, almost a million and a half people sustain a TBI, and 80,000 to 90,000 of them experience a long-term disability as a result.

Many TBIs, like mine, are the result of car accidents; others are caused by falls and assault. TBIs can affect one part of the brain or more than one area, and their severity can range from mild concussions to significant injuries that can result in comas, paralysis, or death. In 2020 alone, more than 64,000 TBI-related deaths were reported by the Centers for Disease Control.

After my initial attempt to stand on my own that day I awoke from my coma, a doctor tried to make clear to me how seriously I'd been injured.

"No one expected you to wake up from your coma," he said, his voice grave. "Statistically you shouldn't be here, since 96 percent of people with your condition pass away."

Later I'd learn that, in the ambulance on the way to the hospital, I "scored" the lowest possible score on the Glasgow Coma Scale, a system developed for assessing the level of consciousness and predicting the ultimate outcome of a coma. A three was the lowest score out of a possible fifteen; I got a three.

The doctor then examined my eyes, telling me that my left pupil was "completely blown" and didn't react to light. This injury would be permanent; my left pupil is dilated to this day.

> *"The brain stem is the central command center for your body. Yours is extremely damaged,"* the doctor said.

"The brain stem," he explained, "is the central command center for your body, controlling breathing, pulse, and body movements. Your brain stem is extremely damaged."

It might be hard for you to picture the brain stem. A wonderful doctor once described it to me this way:

"The brain is like a ball of Silly Putty wrapped around a Popsicle stick. The Popsicle stick represents the spine. The connecting point between the spine and the brain is the brain stem. If something hits the ball of Silly Putty hard enough, it can turn around on the Popsicle stick, slide up and down, tear, and be knocked out of its original shape. The axons that carry messages from the brain stem throughout the body can be severely damaged. That's what happened to your brain."

I'd go on to learn that when my brain stem was severed, the communication between my brain and the left side of my body was shut down. My rehabilitation involved teaching my brain to "talk to" my left side again.

> *I was always on the lookout for the reason I'd had to return from the comfort of heaven.*

It would be an arduous process, infinitely harder than recovering from a painful divorce and more gruelingly strenuous than even the most intense marathon. Recovery would test me emotionally as well as physically. And it would test my spirit.

But the discipline of training for that biathlon prior to the accident helped me go through rehab. I stayed focused on my goals and continued to push myself to achieve them, just as I had when I was preparing for a race. So I trained for walking. I walked a little faster and a little farther during each session of physical therapy. As I had before, I pushed myself to my physical limit. It was humbling, to say the least, to go from sprinting to barely being able to cross a room slowly, but I persevered.

I also was always on the lookout for the reason I'd had to return from the comfort of heaven. I was aware that I was given a second chance at life when so many don't get second chances. I was curious: *What did God have for me to do? What would be my purpose? What would be the answer to my* life's "Why?"

I had a glimpse of what it might be one day during my rehabilitation process. Near the end of my time at the hospital, I shared a room with a young woman who was in a coma. Her husband and preschool-aged son would come visit her every single day.

One day the little boy lingered by the end of my bed.

"Hi," I whispered, sensing he had something to tell me.

"Hi," he said. "You're not asleep."

"No, I'm awake," I said, smiling at him.

"My mommy's sleeping," he said.

"Yes, your mommy is sleeping," I replied. "A few weeks ago, I was sleeping too."

"You were?" he asked, his eyes wide. "Did it hurt?"

"No. I didn't feel any pain while I was sleeping, and your mommy doesn't feel any pain either."

The young boy smiled and ran back to his father, who mouthed "thank you" to me.

Later I'd describe that experience to my mother.

"Mom," I said. "One day I want to be a voice for people who cannot speak."

I had an initial sense that *this*—speaking for those who could not speak and offering comfort to families of survivors—might be the ultimate purpose in my recovery. And confirming this calling, the same doctor who helped me understand the function of the brain stem would later, in one of my bleakest moments, ask me to meet with families of TBI survivors, facilitating weekly trauma support groups, giving families hope when their own situations looked and felt utterly hopeless.

Talking about Heaven

You might think that the moment I was reunited with them, I'd have told my parents about my interaction with their two mothers, Gram and Grandma Sue. But I didn't. It was actually a long time before I felt physically, emotionally, and even spiritually ready to talk about my visit to heaven.

Initially, of course, it was too hard to speak much at all. My throat was sore, my lungs so weak that just breathing took an effort. My attempts to formulate my thoughts and then speak made relaying this experience to them seem nearly impossible.

My parents had already been through so much since the accident, sitting by my bedside, praying for me, worrying about me, disrupting their lives to be at the hospital. What if this news, that I'd been to heaven, disturbed or upset them? That's the last thing I wanted to do.

We'd had a sweet reunion the day I woke up, with my parents expressing that they had faith—throughout the entire time I was in a coma—that I would wake up and recover. In fact, I learned, there came a point a few weeks after the accident when the medical staff caring for me would have chosen to "unplug" me as they thought it would be impossible for me to breathe and function on my own ever again.

Many people thought I'd never even wake up or, if I did, I would awaken with what is known as "unresponsive wakefulness syndrome," where people open their eyes but otherwise don't respond to stimulation and remain unaware of their surroundings. Legally, however, that weighty decision has to be made by the next of kin, and my family demanded that I be put on life support. They continued to pray for a miracle.

"If God wants her to die, then he'll take her home," my dad had told the doctor. "I will not pull the plugs! I have faith that my daughter will be okay. I don't know exactly what shape 'okay' will be, but we'll take it."

To the surprise of everyone, including myself, I ended up being more than "okay." I even was able to run a race six years after the accident and an indoor triathlon at the ten-year anniversary mark! People can't help but be surprised when they hear about the races I've run since my accident. All I can say is, since being in the presence of God in heaven, I believe and have come to know that *nothing* is impossible for Him.

Between waking up from the coma and reaching those stunning goals, though, I battled depression and insomnia, spent countless hours in physical therapy, and worked with social workers and psychologists. I was let go from work. I had to relearn simple bodily tasks, like a toddler, and everything I did took exponentially more energy than it had before. For years, I felt like my body was driving on flat tires.

> *Since being in the presence of God, I have come to know that nothing is impossible for Him.*

But it was only after I had come to terms spiritually with what had happened to me and with what God had in store for my future that I was able to tell my parents about where I was when I was in the coma. A loving nun, Sister Val, helped get me to that point. She was the first person I told about visiting heaven.

I'd sought Sister Val's support before, when I was going through my divorce. So, a few years after the accident, when I found myself in a period of feeling spiritually numb and exhausted and even shut out from God, I returned to her parish office. We met regularly, then, for more than two years, during which time she mostly listened to me. Sister Val is a gifted, deep listener.

Remembering the way I could speak to Sister Val during a time when I found it so hard to talk to others about my feelings continues to inspire me when I talk with other catastrophic injury survivors. I am insistent, telling audiences that no matter what you are going through, it's critical that you communicate and express your feelings. Don't keep them bottled in. Don't lock others out of your life. When you find yourself in a dark place, I tell them, reach out for help.

Some of the first words I spoke to Sister Val were the ones we returned to: "Why me?"

I also confided to her, after describing what heaven was like, that I wished I could have stayed there. Before finally taking the risk of telling her about what happened while I was in the coma, I felt lonely and isolated. I felt the way I imagine the first astronauts felt—a little lost after having had the magnificent experience of going to the moon but returning to earth where no one else had ever experienced what they had. No one understood

I feared no one would understand or even believe me about visiting heaven.

the amazing, otherworldly experience they'd had. And I feared no one would understand or even believe me about visiting heaven.

"I was dead and went to heaven," I confessed to Sister Val. "It was so peaceful there, full of light. I started to walk toward the narrow tunnel with this intense light flowing through it, but my grandmothers stopped me and wouldn't let me go there. I was so disappointed. I wanted to stay."

I described the piercing and all-encompassing blue light that shone through me, around me, and inside me.

"My grandmothers told me that my body would heal," I said. "They said, 'Go back and be happy.' And the next thing I remember is waking up from the coma in the rehab hospital."

"I am sure you wish you were still there," Sister Val said, her voice accepting and kind. She not only believed me, but she seemed to understand why I'd be heartbroken to leave.

I continued. "It's just that I felt so close to God there, and now I feel separated from Him."

I'm not the first person of faith who longed to be in heaven with God instead of living on earth. Even Paul, in the book of Philippians, writes: "I desire to depart and be with Christ, which is better by far" (Philippians 1:23, NIV). But Sister Val reassured me, over and over in our conversations, that God was with me here too.

She also educated me about "survivor's guilt" as she felt I was acutely experiencing it. That is, as I met with other people who had experienced catastrophic injuries, I felt conflicted and, yes, even guilty. I wondered: *Why was I given the gift of so much healing and recovery when others died or lived with far greater disabilities than I did?* Every time I visited with survivors and their families, I saw what *could* have been my life—I could have been left unable to speak, unable to walk, unable to interact with the people I loved.

Why me?

In the end, Sister Val said she couldn't answer my ultimate question of why I survived and even was able to function so well after having a nearly completely severed brain stem. She told me, though, that it was up to me to accept God's gift of this new, different life. I could make choices, she said, about how to humbly accept this blessing and become the person God wanted me to become. After countless hours together, I finally felt ready to accept—fully and with an open, trusting heart—the gift of this second chance that God had given me.

I will never understand why some people survive and heal and others do not, but that's not for me to understand. First Corinthians 13:12 (NIV) reads: "For now we see only a reflection as in a mirror; then we shall see face to face. Now I know in part; then I shall know fully, even as I am fully known." There are many mysteries in this life, so many stories we cannot fully understand. Someday, though, when we are with God, we will have a clear understanding of His ways.

I finally felt freed from the longing to go back to who I had been—that *other* Julie with her invincibility and endless energy—before the accident. I accepted that I had been injured, but I also knew that my identity wasn't "Julie the injured person." I again felt Jesus's presence so very close to me as I had as a little girl.

> *Someday when we are with God, we will have a clear understanding of His ways.*

And in healing spiritually, I finally felt ready to tell my parents about my time in heaven. One afternoon after meeting with Sister Val, I called Mom at her work, telling her I had important news to share. I'd been living on my own for more than a year at this point, and I just couldn't wait until the next time I'd see her to tell her.

"It's about Gram," I said. "I…uh…I saw her in heaven. She looks great. And Grandma Sue was there too."

My words jumbled together as I tried to convey this experience in the light with Mom. I didn't want to upset her, but rather to reassure her that her own mother was okay. *Everything was okay. In fact, it was more than okay.* I also wanted her to know that my body was starting to heal, just like my grandmother told me it would.

"This is comforting to hear," she said. Later, when I spoke to both of my parents at their home, more fully telling them about my experience in heaven, they said they suspected that I had been with the Lord while I was in the coma.

"You just seemed so peaceful," they said.

But, on the phone that day, I could hear my mom's muffled tears.

"It means a lot to know my mother's okay in heaven. And Julie," she added, her voice shaking, "I'm *so* glad that you're okay."

That identity thief no longer had me under its control; I had accepted the new version of who I was.

I was healing, inside and out.

Forgiveness

Part of my healing journey and becoming the person God wanted me to be involved another difficult task: forgiving the driver who had run that red light and caused the accident. I'd looked at the young man's name and read his phone number countless times. I kept the police report perched on top of my dresser.

Deep in my heart, I knew I would need to face the past so I could move into the future. The Holy Spirit gently nudged me, reminding me that forgiving would release me from pain and having to carry heavy spiritual baggage. Ever since I was a child, I'd learned from my parents and from my Catholic education how vital forgiveness is, how it's the centerpiece of the Christian faith.

All through Scripture, we learn that God's forgiveness is not about what a person deserves, but about the loving character of God Himself. In Matthew 18:21–22 (NIV), when Peter asks Jesus how often he must forgive—"up to seven times?"—Jesus answers, "I tell you, not seven times, but seventy-seven times."

After I awoke from the coma and realized what had happened, I was aware of not seventy-seven, but just one act of forgiveness I would need to make someday. And, almost one year after the accident, I finally felt ready to do it. Before then, my heart would cloud with anger and confusion when I thought of the person who had so profoundly injured me.

> *As my body healed, God's Holy Spirit had been at work in my soul, releasing me from the anger.*

But all along as my body healed, God's Holy Spirit had been at work in my soul, releasing me from this anger so that I could be spiritually healed.

Finally, one day I picked up the phone, and praying, dialed the number I'd read countless times on the report. A man's voice answered, and I asked, "Is this Robert?" (This is not his real name.) After he said it was, I continued.

Dialing the phone to speak with the teenager who ran into my car was difficult. I had harbored feelings of bitterness against him. His irresponsible decision to speed through a red light upended my life and caused great suffering. His actions took away my physical ability to hold down a full-time job. I could no longer count on my body to work the way it used to.

However, I realized that for my healing to progress, I had to speak with him. I needed to hear myself forgive him.

"Hello, Robert," I said. "This is Julie Papievis."

As soon as I said my name, Robert exclaimed, "Oh, Julie! I never knew what happened to you. You were still in the coma when I went to traffic court. No one would tell me anything. I always think about you."

"Well, Robert," I said. "I have been thinking a lot about you too. That's why—"

He then interrupted me, clearly anguished.

"Julie, before you say anything, I have to say something. I am *so* sorry for what I did to you. I am so sorry."

"I forgive you, Robert," I said, my voice strong and determined. "That's why I called. I've waited a long time to hear myself say that to you."

After I spoke those words, he was silent for a few moments. Robert and I had been suffering in silence, each with our own private burdens. Finally, we had the unique opportunity to comfort each other and to help the other heal. He gave me the gift of his sincere apology. I received it and gave him the gift of forgiveness. It was a powerful moment.

Finally, he broke the silence and said, "Tell me about what happened to you."

I tried not to focus on what I knew to be the consequences *he'd* faced after the accident: a ticket with a $75 fine.

"Do you *really* want to know?" I asked.

He said he did.

"Well," I said. "I had to start over and relearn how to do everything from swallowing to standing up."

I described my rehabilitation in detail and said that I was still going each week for physical and occupational therapy. I'd spent about a month in intensive care after the accident, then was transferred to the rehab hospital, where after about a month I woke up. I'd spend another two months there before being released to my parents' house.

There was no way to summarize all I'd been through: how I'd had double pneumonia when I was in the coma, how I'd lost my job and sense of self, what it felt like to endure intense pain, and the unease of living with my parents again like a child for a month after rehab, having to ring a bell to call them in so they could help me use the toilet, or that I would never be a mother.

I couldn't begin to explain what the emotional pain was like, how although there were no obvious scars, nothing a passerby would notice, on the inside, my spirit had been broken. I had to deal with and ulti-mately accept the reality that I was living in a body that didn't feel or work like the one I had before.

> *I had to ultimately accept the reality that I was living in a body that didn't feel or work like the one I had before.*

My brain skimmed over countless other humiliations and losses. But I knew I had forgiven him, by the grace of God, so I had to let all of this go. So I simply asked, "Don't you think it would be a good idea to include community service in a rehabilitation facility as part of a court sentence? That way, drivers can understand and experience the impact of their choices."

He agreed that would be a very good idea.

"Julie," he said, his tone somber, "I want you to know that I'm such a careful driver now."

"I'm glad. I'm sure you've had your own issues to deal with too," I said. "I wish you all the best. I really do. And I will pray for you."

After he thanked me, I decided to say something more.

"I had to call and talk to you," I said. "I wanted to let you know that I'll be okay. You don't have to carry the burden of wondering what happened. God has given me an amazing gift. Robert, I've forgiven you, so now it's time that you forgave yourself."

Hanging up the phone, I felt my shoulders relax. I felt the warmth of God's love fill my heart. I felt gratitude. Through the act of forgiveness, any anger that had been poisoning my heart evaporated. Another part of me was ready to be healed.

The Dutch physician and botanist Paul Boese once said, "Forgiveness does not change the past, but it does enlarge the future." I knew my future would be more expansive after I forgave Robert. My prayer is that his future has been enlarged too.

An Expansive Future

I firmly believe we all have a future, one that God has planned. Perhaps you've experienced great pain and loss and you can't imagine what the coming years will hold. Perhaps they will be nothing like the ones you had in mind, but they are still your future. And they have been orchestrated by God.

One of my favorite verses is Jeremiah 29:11 (NIV), which reads, "For I know the plans I have for you," declares the LORD, "plans to prosper you and not to harm you, plans to give you hope and a future."

This message is reiterated and developed by author and pastor Rick Warren. He starts his book *The Purpose Driven Life* by saying, "It's not about you. The purpose of your life is far greater than your own personal fulfillment, your peace of mind, or even your happiness. It's far greater than your family, your career, or even your wildest dreams and ambitions. If you want to know why you were placed on this planet, you must begin with God. You were born by His purpose and for His purpose."

Isn't that powerful? God has plans, hope, and a future for each of us. I hold tight to that promise every day. We don't have control over how long our lives will be, but every single day is a gift, waiting to be unwrapped and enjoyed.

> *We don't have control over how long our lives will be, but every single day is a gift.*

People often ask me: "So, how do I find my calling? My future?"

I tell them: Pray. Speak to God like He is really listening because He is. Reach out to friends and family who can help support you along the way. Acknowledge your feelings and accept your circumstances and condition.

Forgive the people who have really disappointed you before, during, and after what happened. Forgive yourself. Ask for God's help in the difficult act of forgiveness. Often, we can't do it on our own.

Face your greatest fears. Be prepared to fail in order to move forward to your future. Be flexible, because we don't always know what happens in life. Find the fortitude to believe in yourself, to believe that you can go beyond your disabling injury or illness. And, yes, make a financial and medical plan to help provide for your future.

And, if you're like me, you can also look forward to your heavenly future! The Bible promises that those who believe in God will experience a life after death. Though the specifics remain a mystery to many of us who are still living, people like me who have gotten a glimpse of heaven are even more expectant for the afterlife.

I believe that I will be raised with Jesus after I die. I will return to that beautiful light, and now, in addition to Gram and Grandma Sue, I know my dad, who died in 2018, will be there to greet me too.

Living with God

God continues to provide strength and remains faithful to me. I am amazed by what my body can do, and that's what I focus on. There's a song little kids sing in Sunday school called "Jesus Loves Me." It begins:

> Jesus loves me, this I know, For the Bible tells me so.
> Little ones to Him belong, We are weak but He is strong.
> Yes, Jesus loves me, Yes, Jesus loves me,
> Yes, Jesus loves me, The Bible tells me so.

It aligns with a passage in the Bible that, since the accident, deeply resonates with me. In 2 Corinthians, Paul writes about a "thorn" that causes him weakness and suffering.

Biblical scholars give a variety of explanations of what this affliction could have been: Chronic pain? Persecution from others? A certain sin he found difficult to conquer? We don't know what Paul's "thorn" was, but when I read, "…for Christ's sake, I delight in weaknesses, in insults, in hardships, in persecutions, in difficulties. For when I am weak, then I am strong" (2 Corinthians 12:10, NIV), I feel a surge of empathy and hope regarding my *own* weakness

Because of my injury, I can never forget how much I must rely on God. I, too, must always be completely dependent on Him to help me wake up and live each day. Because I remain weak, His power is made perfect. Because of Him, I walk. Because of Him, I run. Because of Him and only with His help, I live.

At the beginning of this story, I quoted the children's book *The Little Prince* and the phrase "what is essential is invisible to the eyes." Now I want to share the whole quote with you. It reads: "It is only with the heart that one can see rightly; what is essential is invisible to the eyes."

> *After my experience visiting heaven, I see this life with my heart and not just with my eyes.*

After my experience visiting heaven, returning to my life here to heal, forgiving the person who altered the course of my life and reconnecting with and becoming fully reliant upon Jesus, I see this life with my heart and not just with my eyes. And I am deeply grateful for all of it—even the accident and subsequent challenges—that have made me the Julie I am today.

Am I happy? Yes. Trust me, I'm not living a "happily ever after" scenario, but who is? I have inner joy. It has been a long journey, but I arrived at a place where I can punctuate my joy with an exclamation point!

My Life since My Near-Death Experience

Julie Papievis

Because of God, I have had the honor of bringing hope and His message of love to thousands of people. Over the past miraculous thirty years, I've had a sense of purpose very different from the one I had when I was in my twenties.

Q *You said that people ask if you "did go back and be happy" like your grandmother instructed you to do. Although your answer is "yes," how has your life been on a daily basis?*

A Given that I'm a person who always tries to tell the *whole* truth, I add that life hasn't been easy.

In my discussion of TBI as a metaphorical "identity thief," I quoted a survivor of TBI who said, "The worst part is…people can't see it." And that continues to be the case for me. I often feel like I'm carrying around a secret, and that secret is about the internal disabilities that I have.

I'm sure I look like I am thriving and, of course, in many ways I am. But that's not the whole story. A stranger might see me park in a handicapped parking spot, for instance, and wonder if I truly belong there. They can't know that, every moment when I'm not lying down, I'm battling vertigo and never have a true sense of balance. It takes me great effort to walk in a straight line, to coordinate my muscles to walk upright and work together. The simplest movements of my body require intentional mental and physical effort. They don't know the extent to which my left side has atrophied.

Since the accident and arriving at the rehab center, in a coma, with pneumonia, my lungs remain weakened and I'm at risk, always, of a recurrence. I have a permanent visual disability, weakness on my left side, and of course, there is much more that I navigate on a daily basis.

Q *If you could turn back time and take the accident away from your life, would you?*

A I can sincerely say that I wouldn't change a thing. If the accident had not happened, I would not know what I know today, and I would not be who I am today. I would not have this sense of deep and gratifying purpose.

And by that, I don't mean that my brain stem injury defines who I am. I don't see myself as a statistic or simply as a "TBI survivor." The accident is something that *happened* to me. My true identity and purpose was given to me by my Lord.

Q *What kind of work do you do to further a message of hope, perseverance, and God's love?*

A I continue to work with the Brain Injury Association, the Spinal Cord Injury Association, and the ThinkFirst Injury Prevention program. I've volunteered in rehab hospitals, and using my accounting and finance education, I serve as a brand ambassador for a wealth management firm. I've worked with countless military veterans, survivors of TBIs, and people with severe PTSD. And I am always able to share with the people I meet that they are beloved of God, just as they are. Even—or even *especially*—when they feel weak.

◦⟋⟍◦

Q *Any future plans you'd like to share about your work or storytelling?*

A My hope is that someday, and if it's God's will, my story will be made into a documentary film. I'd love to share my message of hope and God's loving presence in that format with audiences.

More Stories of
Heavenly Encounters

By Editors of Guideposts

Inside the Book

By Lori Sciame

I stood in my office, surrounded by books. They were everywhere! Piled on my desk, stacked in cardboard boxes on the floor. There had to be hundreds of them. I had no idea that the children's book drive I'd organized at work would be so successful, and I hoped I hadn't taken on too much too soon.

Of course, I shouldn't have been surprised. My coworkers were kind, caring people. I'd experienced that kindness firsthand a few years ago, after my cancer diagnosis.

One morning, while getting ready for work, I'd found a lump in my breast. I scheduled an appointment with the doctor immediately. Cancer ran in my family, and I wasn't going to take any chances. A mammogram found six tumors. I had Stage III breast cancer.

When I broke the news at the office, everyone offered their love and support. Especially Kathy. She pulled me aside. "Anything you need," she said, "please don't hesitate to ask. I don't want you to feel alone during this."

Kathy was true to her word. When chemo left me too drained to cook, Kathy organized a potluck and brought ready-made meals to my house. When the lifesaving radiation compromised my immune system, Kathy's daughter sewed me a cloth face mask to wear to my doctor appointments—pink, for breast cancer. Kathy and I grew closer, and on the days when I was well enough to go into the office, we'd stop by each other's desks to talk.

During one of our chats, I learned why Kathy knew exactly what I needed. Her mother had also had cancer. "She died when I was young," she said. "I still miss her every day."

I tried to reassure her that mother-daughter love endures even death, that her mother was always with her in spirit. But I knew words would never be enough. I wished there was something I could do to return even a fraction of the comfort Kathy had given to me, but how? Only the Lord could bring Kathy the peace she needed, and I prayed for that every day. It gave me something else to focus on.

After thirteen rounds of chemo, I was healing from my surgeries, wrapping up the radiation treatments and able to go into work more often. I found my energy finally returning. Before I'd gotten sick, I'd loved to organize company fundraisers and community outreach. Now I was feeling up to it again.

That's how the book drive came about. There were little free libraries all over town, drop-off points where people could give away books to those who needed them. I wanted to stock them with children's books. And though I was overjoyed by the number of donations from my coworkers and their friends and families, sorting through the books was overwhelming. As I was moving some of them off my chair to take a breather, Shane, the building's maintenance man, entered my office carrying even more books.

"Look!" he said, holding up a Harry Potter book. "Doesn't Kathy love this series?"

"She does, and we've already gotten a few copies of it."

"Why don't I put this one on her desk then?" he said. "As a little gift.

I agreed. Caught up in going through box after box of books, I forgot all about it. Until the next day, when Kathy tracked me down, tears in her eyes. "Lori, did you leave this on my desk?" she asked, clutching the copy of Harry Potter.

"Shane found it in the donations. We thought you'd like it. Why? Is something wrong?"

Kathy opened the book to the title page, holding it out for me to see. There was a handwritten inscription: "To Donna, Love Sarah, Happy Birthday." There was a heart drawn next to it.

"This is my mother's handwriting!" Kathy said. "Donna and Sarah are my sisters. Sarah was too young to sign the book herself, so Mom did it for her."

Kathy went on to explain that the book was one of the last gifts her mom had given. The three sisters had cherished the handwriting in it. Over the years, the book had been misplaced. None of them knew what had happened to it. Yet somehow, here it was. Out of hundreds of books donated from countless households in and around Phoenix, Arizona, this long-lost treasure had made it back into the right hands. Offering peace to the woman who'd comforted me through my journey. Reminding us both that there is no journey we travel alone.

Tracks in the Snow

By Gena Wilimitis

---◆---

Thick snowflakes swirled around my windshield. Everything around me was blanketed in white. The light was fading as the sun set over the rocky peaks.

I was driving up a mountain pass on what was supposed to be a four-hour trip from Red River, New Mexico, to Durango, Colorado. I inched along on a winding, unfamiliar road in a snowstorm.

I was on my way to meet my boyfriend, who was visiting his family in Durango. He'd invited me to join them for the weekend. I was staying at a friend's house in Red River. The fastest way to Durango from Red River would take me through this mountain road, but I was so excited about the weekend ahead that the route didn't faze me. I left without checking the weather.

Thirty minutes into my drive, the snow had started. Gentle flurries at first. I thought about turning around. But it hardly looked threatening, so I continued.

Now I regretted that decision. But it was too late. The road was too narrow and icy for me to turn around. To my right was a sheer cliff face, and to the left, a sharp drop-off descending hundreds of feet. The snow was bad, getting worse. The only way out was forward, higher and higher into the mountains. The last bit of sunlight disappeared, and I couldn't see anything beyond the few feet illuminated by my headlights. I panicked.

My cell phone had lost service as soon as I'd entered the mountain pass and remained at zero bars. I couldn't call for help. I had some bottled water in the trunk. The clothes in my luggage. Maybe I could find a place to pull over and bundle up until morning. Would that be enough to keep me warm all night? How long would it take for someone to find me? If anyone ever would. I gripped the wheel tighter.

"Please, God, help me," I whispered.

Then I noticed something. A pair of lights seemed to glow dimly through the snowstorm. I blinked hard, then peered ahead. There they were. Taillights! There was a car in front of me! At least someone was here with me. *Focus on the lights,* I told myself, *not your fear.*

I followed my guide for at least another half hour as we continued to ascend the mountain. Finally, I felt the road start to level out and then gradually descend. I lost sight of the taillights ahead of me. But the panic didn't return. I could see the car's tire tracks in my headlights. All I had to do was follow the tracks the rest of the way down the mountain.

I drove slowly, keeping my wheels within the tracks every inch of the way. Soon I could see the lights of a town twinkling in the distance. The snow started to cover the tracks I was following. But both of us had made it.

At the base of the mountain, I spotted taillights. I wondered if it was my guide. If so, I wanted to thank him. But as I got closer, I saw it wasn't a car. It was a snowplow. I pulled up beside it and rolled down my window. The driver of the plow did the same.

"Excuse me," I said. "Did you see another car come down this road, ahead of me?"

The driver looked at me as if I was insane. "Lady," he said, "I don't know what you're talking about. I've been working here at the base of the mountain for the past two or three hours. No one has gone up or come down that mountain but you."

I didn't correct him, but I knew differently. I hadn't been alone on that mountain road that night.

Heaven's Stadium

By Wanda R. Martin

It was past midnight. I'd been lying in the dark for half an hour, unable to sleep. My mind was on my late husband, Hardy. I squeezed my eyes shut. *God, please give me some kind of sign that Hardy is okay.*

Hardy's passing had been so traumatic that, six months after he passed, I still wondered if he was at peace. The weekend Hardy had died of a heart attack, I was in Michigan doing a gig with my singing group. When I got home on Sunday, I found him on our bedroom floor. It was too late. He was already gone. "Help!" I hollered and ran out of the room, out of the house. My neighbors were there in a flash, holding me, comforting me. They took care of everything over the next few days. After his death, I never went back into our bedroom. I slept on the sofa until I was able to sell our house and move.

Hardy's passing left a huge hole in my life. In addition to being my spouse of forty-three years, he was my business partner and my best friend. For much of our married life, we'd had a communications company that designed audio systems for large spaces, such as airports and stadiums. We traveled to venues all over the world for work. Wherever we were, he'd always find me toward the end of the day. "I'll be home soon," he'd say, winking. It was an inside joke, a way to acknowledge that we never actually left each other's side to go to our respective jobs. That daily check-in reminded me of the connection we shared.

I turned on my side, trying to get comfortable. I missed Hardy so much. I longed to see him, to hear his voice. I wanted to know that he was okay. I wanted to say goodbye. Eventually, I fell asleep.

Then I was dreaming. I was walking down a long hallway in a big stadium, just like the stadiums Hardy and I worked in. At the end, I found myself in the seats, about six levels up. I looked to my right, and leaning against a concrete support wall was a dear friend who worked for us for decades.

She was smiling and nodding, as if to affirm that I was going in the right direction. To my left, sitting on a platform near the aisle, was my husband's best friend, who'd passed about a year before Hardy did. He was working an audio board. He just nodded his head, smiling. He signaled that he wanted me to follow his gaze. I did, and across the aisle and up a level, standing behind an audio console and smiling down at me, was Hardy! He looked better than when I'd last seen him. His hair was no longer gray but dark brown, like it was when we'd first met. He was positively radiant. I felt a powerful love wash over me. Hardy walked down the stairs in front of me. He came up to me, wrapped his arms around me, and kissed me.

Then he looked into my eyes and said, "I'll be home soon."

I awoke the next morning, smiling at the lingering memory of the dream. My prayers had been heard. Not only was Hardy okay, but our connection endured. To heaven and back.

Invisible World

By Chamisa Loraine Howard

I believe most people will get to witness one big miracle in their lifetime. Something so incredible, it leaves you forever changed. That miracle happened to me on April 23, 1959, in North Hollywood, California, an ordinary Thursday.

I was nineteen. The mother of a toddler with another on the way—and soon. I was nine months pregnant. I should've been lying on the couch, avoiding stress. But stress I had in spades. Not only was I looking after my son—eighteen-month-old Vern—but my mother had roped me into babysitting for three of my younger siblings: two-year-old Hugh, five-year-old Lolly, and fourteen-year-old Danny. I was the oldest of ten kids, so that happened a lot. Danny could take care of himself, but the other three kids were a handful—rambunctious and as curious as cats. They got into everything. Keeping an eye on them was a full-time job. Which was why I remembered I hadn't put the trash out only as I heard the garbage truck rumbling down the road.

"Watch the kids for me!" I called to Danny before hurrying outside, latching the screen door behind me. I flagged down the approaching truck.

Waddling, I dragged the trash can out to the road in front of our house. If you could call it a house. My husband had recently enrolled at

California State University, Northridge. A friend in the administration had set us up with free housing at a beautiful new place, still under construction. Until it was ready, we needed a place to stay. A cheap place to stay. The rent at this ramshackle place was only $50 a month. *It's only temporary,* I told myself.

There were many things to hate about the house. With its cement floors and unfinished interior, I'd had to do some serious work to make it homey. I'd painted the walls, put up curtains and covered the cement floors with rugs. But the thing that unnerved me most was our proximity to the train tracks. The Southern Pacific Railroad ran right through our backyard, a mere fifty feet from our back door. It was the railroad that connected the farming communities along the Pacific Coast to big cities like San Francisco and Los Angeles. The huge, noisy steam engines rattled by every twenty minutes—so punctual you could set your watch by them—shaking the walls of the house as they did.

Like most toddlers, my son, Vern, and brother Hugh were fascinated by the trains. Whenever they heard its whistle, they'd run to the back screen door, pressing their noses against it so hard, they'd come away with crisscross marks on their foreheads. They'd squeal, pointing at the "choo-choos." The whole thing made me nervous. There was nothing but an expanse of grass bordering a cow pasture and an old gnarled mulberry tree separating the back door from the tracks.

Watching the garbage truck rumble away, I heard a familiar whistle. The 4 p.m. train, right on time. I turned back to the house, then stopped.

There was something different about the train's whistle. Instead of a short blow, like the conductors usually gave as they passed, this was a long, agonized wail. Along with the metallic shriek of a speeding train trying—and failing—to brake.

Every fiber in my being screamed one thing: Vern! Hugh!

I tore around the corner of the house. The tracks were in plain view. And so were Vern and Hugh. They were standing in the middle of the tracks! Pointing happily at the on- coming train.

Where was Danny? How had the boys gotten out of the house? I'd latched the door, unless . . . Lolly! My little sister was just tall enough to open the latch.

I raced for the tracks, screaming, desperately trying to get to the boys. I heard the screen door fling open behind me. "What's the matter?" Danny said.

"The boys!" I cried. "Train tracks!"

Danny took off. He was an athletic boy—much faster than I could be nine months pregnant. He ran past me. But it was no use—the train wasn't going to brake in time. Sparks flew from where the wheels bit into the metal tracks, like a fireworks display on the Fourth of July.

"Vern! Hugh! Move!" I screamed.

They couldn't hear me. They were too mesmerized by the choo-choo barreling toward them. The horrific scene played out in my mind's eye.

I was going to watch my son die! My brother die!

What happened was so sudden, I wasn't sure if I was in shock. The scene in front of me shifted, ever so slightly and a figure appeared, out of nothing, on the side of the tracks. As if something invisible had suddenly become visible. It was a man wearing a neatly pressed brown suit and blue shirt, no tie. Before I could yell for his help, he scooped the

boys off the tracks. A second later, the train rocketed by, whistle screaming, brakes shrieking.

Danny and I reached the tracks, eyes wide and panting. The man
handed the boys to us, then just like that, face, hands, and body disappeared into nothingness again. As if he'd never been there. As if we
weren't supposed to see him.

The train faded from sight. Danny and I carried the boys back,
speechless. *They weren't even wearing shoes,* I thought. That night, when
my husband came home, I went to the tracks. I studied the spot where
it had happened. Something was stuck between the rails. A pair of pow-
der blue sneakers and a pair of little white sandals. Hugh and Vern had
been lifted right out of their shoes.

Vern and Hugh—now grown with children of their own—don't
remember that day. They were too young. But Danny and I will never
forget.

That moment when, for an instant, the veil was lifted on an invisible
world, and the forces at work that protect us.

Not Alone

By Joe O'Brien

———— ◆◆ ————

T he phone rang late one night. It was my brother Kerry.

"Joe, Sammy's plane was shot down during the air strike," he said.

Sammy, our mutual friend, was a lieutenant colonel and fighter pilot with the Kuwait Air Force. Kerry quickly filled me in on the details. Sammy was alive, but he was being held prisoner. He'd been badly beaten. We didn't know what would happen to him next or whether he'd even make it out.

At that point, I'd known Sammy for about twelve years. I met him through Kerry, who lived in Saudi Arabia and had friends all over the world. One summer, he invited Sammy to come with him to California when he returned home to visit. Sammy and I instantly hit it off. We'd both been in the Air Force and were familiar with the same fighters, specifically the A4 Skyhawk, which he flew. He was kind and easy to be around. Someone I was proud to call my friend.

I got off the phone with Kerry and switched on the news to try to get some more information. There weren't any further updates, so I decided to go to bed. I tossed and turned for a while.

Eventually, I fell asleep. I had the strangest, most realistic dream. I was in a dark room. I innately knew I was viewing everything through

Sammy's eyes. There was a small window high up on the wall with a dim light hanging above it. I could just barely see the maroon porcelain-tiled walls. It was so cold in the room that my body convulsed with shivers.

And I felt intense pain in my hands. It radiated from the base of my thumbs and encircled my wrists. I was clinging to a green-and-white-striped blanket, and for some reason, it felt significant. A comfort amid the desolation.

I woke up the next morning with the dream still clear in my mind.

It made sense to be dreaming about Sammy, but why all those tactile details? Sammy had been captured in the hot desert. In my worst imaginings I'd pictured him in a stifling concrete cell, not a cold room with tiled walls. I didn't understand the significance of the striped blanket. Or the pain in my wrists.

I sat up in bed, pulled back the covers, and winced. What in the world? My wrists were sore, as if the pain from the dream had traveled into real life. I jumped up and ran to the bathroom. Splashed cold water on my face. Ran it over my hands. The pain ebbed a bit, but it was definitely real. It was so acute that I had trouble holding things for five days.

The whole experience was so strange that I kept it to myself while we waited for news. Finally, about a month later, Kerry called. Sammy was being released! He called from the hospital once he'd had some rest, and I talked to him for a bit. Told him how happy I was that he was okay. He sounded tired but in good spirits. We stayed in touch throughout his recovery, but it was another two years before we saw each other again.

Sammy and his sister came to my family's home for the holidays. It was a joyous reunion. Along with my daughters, Kathleen and Amy, I greeted them at the door with cheers and hugs. We all sat down in the kitchen to catch up. Eventually the conversation turned to Sammy's imprisonment. I'd never intended to tell Sammy about my dream. I didn't want to remind him of such a traumatic time in his life. But since the topic had come up, I felt compelled to share what had happened.

I told Sammy about the small window, the dimly lit walls, my wrists hurting, and the white blanket with green stripes. I half expected Sammy to tell me I was crazy. But when I was done, he looked amazed. Then he talked about what happened during his imprisonment, sharing details that he'd never told anyone.

The room he was kept in had one small window high on the wall with a light hanging above it. It had maroon tile walls. His captors had cuffed his hands so tightly that his wrists were cut and caused him great pain. He pulled up his sleeves to show me the scars. The room had been dark and miserably cold. His only comfort was a thin blanket with green and white stripes.

We stared at each other in silence. Everything matched. From halfway around the world, I'd actually seen Sammy's imprisonment. But how?

Sammy and I don't have all the answers, but we both know that in the darkest time of his life, he wasn't alone. The bonds of friendship truly are mysterious. And all of us are spiritually connected in ways that transcend earthly comprehension.

The "Wrong" Mrs. McCarthy

By Sister Josephine Palmeri

ammy McCarthy entered the classroom at the Catholic high school where I teach, fighting back tears.

That was strange. Tammy was normally such a bubbly, happy girl. Instead of taking her usual seat, she approached my desk. "Sister Josephine," she said, her voice wavering, "would you pray for my mother? She went to the hospital with chest pains this morning."

"Of course, I will!" I said. "Which hospital? Can she have visitors?"

Tammy perked up a bit. "Oh, it would be great if you stopped by," she said. "Mom would appreciate that. She's at Moses Taylor Hospital."

"Then I'll be there."

That evening, my friend Sister Angeline and I arrived at the hospital. I carried a card I'd drawn myself—a picture of a smiling nun. "Dear Mrs. McCarthy," I'd written in my neatest handwriting, "the sisters are praying for you."

"We're here to see a Mrs. McCarthy," I told the woman at the hospital's reception desk.

"Just a moment," the receptionist said. "We have a June McCarthy in Room 310."

We thanked her and headed to Room 310. But as soon as I saw the woman sitting in the bed, I knew it must've been a mistake. This had to be the wrong Mrs. McCarthy. There was no way this woman had a daughter still in high school. She looked to be in her late sixties.

"Mrs. McCarthy?" I asked.

"That's me!" she boomed.

Her voice belied her slight frame. I had no idea how such a small woman could project so loudly. "Come in! I just told God I need company and he sends me two nuns. Imagine that!"

June had bone cancer. It had started in her jaw but had spread. "It's like having a toothache in every tooth in your mouth!" June said. "But no more complaining out of me!"

She kept us entertained for more than an hour with stories, her blue eyes shining with good humor. June had certainly led an interesting life. She lived in Scranton, in an apartment above a tavern. "When I get out of here, you two need to come visit me," she said. "We'll go down to the bar for a snorkie."

"What's a snorkie?" I asked.

"A shot of whiskey," she laughed

We promised we'd visit when she was released. As we left, she said, "You know, talking to you made me forget the pain."

Sister Angeline and I exchanged glances. There was no need to mention we'd meant to visit someone else. On the way out, we checked with the receptionist—there was no other Mrs. McCarthy in the hospital. The next day, Tammy told us her mother has been released before we'd arrived. We had indeed visited the wrong Mrs. McCarthy.

But Sister Angeline and I kept our word. When June was eventually released from the hospital, we paid her a visit. Her apartment was small but charming, full of little knickknacks and treasures. She collected ceramic elephants, though only ones with their trunks raised skyward.

"If an elephant's trunk is turned up, that's good luck," she told us. "If not, uh-oh!"

June was a delightful hostess. She served us strawberry shortcake as she regaled us with bawdy jokes. The woman could have been a comedian! All she needed was an audience—and a little company.

Our visits became a regular thing. Oftentimes her sister, Ruth, would be there too. As the months passed, June had less and less energy and needed more assistance, but she never lost her spark. In nice weather, she'd sit on the little bench on her tiny landing.

Even after the cancer stole June's ability to speak and she was confined to a hospital bed, she was still as "talkative" as ever, communicating through written notes. And though June insisted we were the ones cheering her up, she always kept us in stitches.

"June," I joked on one visit, "if you suddenly feel well enough to go out, don't forget, you owe me a snorkie!" She nodded, her blue eyes crinkling with silent laughter.

That was the last time I saw my friend. A few days after that visit, Ruth called to let me know that June had passed peacefully in her sleep. In the months we'd known each other, in all the conversations we had, I'd never once mentioned that our first meeting wasn't something I had planned. That Sister Angeline and I had entered the room of the wrong Mrs. McCarthy. In my heart, I knew she was the right one.

A Note from the Editors

We hope you enjoyed *A Place of Light and Love*, published by Guideposts. For over 75 years, Guideposts, a nonprofit organization, has been driven by a vision of a world filled with hope. We aspire to be the voice of a trusted friend, a friend who makes you feel more hopeful and connected.

By making a purchase from Guideposts, you join our community in touching millions of lives, inspiring them to believe that all things are possible through faith, hope, and prayer. Your continued support allows us to provide uplifting resources to those in need. Whether through our communities, websites, apps, or publications, we inspire our audiences, bring them together, and comfort, uplift, entertain, and guide them. Visit us at guideposts.org to learn more.

We would love to hear from you. Write us at Guideposts, P.O. Box 5815, Harlan, Iowa 51593 or call us at (800) 932-2145. Did you love *A Place of Light and Love?* Leave a review for this product on guideposts.org/shop. Your feedback helps others in our community find relevant products.

Find inspiration, find faith, find Guideposts.
Shop our best sellers and favorites at
guideposts.org/shop
Or scan the QR code to go directly to our Shop